Praise for *Swampoodle Lily*

"In this very careful and extensive study of the artistry of St. Aloysius Church, Mr. Bob Murray has brought together history, poetry, wonderful photography and his own extensive knowledge of art and architecture, to enable his reader to share his enthrallment with the genius of both Constantino Brumidi, the great Washington master artist and Fr. Benedict, Sestini, S.J., Jesuit architect and astronomer, a genius enshrined by them in this holy edifice which for almost two centuries has captivated and inspired generations of Catholic parishioners and Gonzaga high school students.

Mr. Murray's research leads us back through the earliest years of St. Aloysius Gonzaga Church and traces thoughtfully its periods of 'prosperity' and decline up to the present, allowing us to see and feel the glory and the pain of each era of this Church's remarkable history, a history continuing today with its most recent lovely renewal and with its latest trial, the roof-raising tornado of 2017."

—*Lucien Longtin, S.J., Spiritual Director, The Jesuit Center, Wernersville, PA.*

"Still standing, firmly planted for over 150 years, St. Aloysius Church, located on the campus of Gonzaga in Washington, D.C., defies the torture of its swampy footing and once again celebrates the genius of its Architect, Benedict Sestini, S.J. and its Master Artist, Constantino Brumidi, and a determined team of conservators.

Author of *Swampoodle Lily*, Robert Murray, along with others on the conservation team tread in and out of St. Aloysius Church's murky setting from 1991-1994 and amazingly and masterfully saved the vintage church restoring it to active use on the Gonzaga campus. Successful fundraising demanded the author dig out and uncover the building's original to the present day structural details and share detailed accounts of its cultural and religious value from its founding to the present. Murray credits the conservation success to its patron, Aloysius Gonzaga, the Patron of Integrity, Stability, and the Dignity of young people today. Once again stable in its urban surroundings, thanks to its ingenious redesign and reconstruction and with the continued blessings by Gonzaga, historic St. Aloysius Church stands securely for many generations to come welcoming all for worship, respite, and a closer look at timeless D.C. history. Author Robert Murray dug literally and physically to save St. Aloysius Church and share its story with you."

—*Anne Ridder, Assistant Dean (Retired), Liberal Studies Program,*
Georgetown University.

"In this world where tourists chase around the globe to appreciate man-made wonders before they disappear from age, neglect or abuse, it is a comfort to discover Robert Murray's book about the design and history of the Church of St. Aloysius Gonzaga in Washington, D.C. Here is a lesser wonder in our own backyard mostly overlooked.

In his own way, Murray preserves the Church with his authoritative description of its network of links to many of the leading forces of art and architecture of the time. William Thornton, Architect of the Capitol, for example, included in the Capitol paintings and decor of the Italian immigrant, Constantino Brumidi, who at the same time was working on the interior of Saint Aloysius, supervising the same artisans who were doing decorative painting in the Capitol.

Murray, an art dealer himself, embellishes his narrative with renditions of the art and architecture of the Church of Saint Aloysius by artist, Nathan Leibowitz, whom Murray commissioned to do the drawings.

It would be a great cultural loss if some day Saint Aloysius is turned into a parking lot. If that happens, Murray's book will be a valuable record of past glory. Meanwhile, tourists visiting Washington, D.C. will find the book an excellent guide to one of the City's unknown pasts."

—*William F. McDonald, Professor, Department of Sociology,*
Georgetown University.

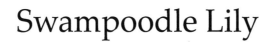

Swampoodle Lily

Swampoodle Lily

Swampoodle Lily

The Jesuit Church of Saint Aloysius Gonzaga.
Reflections on Some of Its Times, Its Growth
and Survival to the Present

Text and Verses by
Robert Francis Murray

Washington DC

Printed in the United States of America

Library of Congress Control Number: 2019933432
ISBN 978-0-9995572-8-0 paperback (alk. paper)
ISBN 978-0-9995572-9-7 hardcover (alk. paper)

 An imprint of New Academia Publishing

 4401-A Connecticut Ave., NW #236 - Washington DC 20008
info@newacademia.com - www.newacademia.com

All illustrations are courtesy of the author, if not otherwise indicated.

May this book bring insights
expressed by Origen (185-252 A.D.)

…that we will begin to see
in visible things those which are invisible,
based not solely upon present realities alone
but on blessings to come…

Abstraction of Interior Stairwell, by James Sanders

Contents

List of Graphics/Visuals

xvi

Introduction

Some seventy plus years ago on a September morning in 1949, I hopped off the streetcar in front of Saint Aloysius Church on North Capitol Street and trooped up the alley between the church and the then Notre Dame Academy to begin my first day as a freshman at Gonzaga College High School. That was my first time seeing the imposing building of Saint Aloysius Church on the Gonzaga campus just a few blocks from the U.S. Capitol building.

Over the years my admiration for the church structure and my curiosity increased to a point in nineteen ninety-three when I was privileged to co-chair as the Director of Aesthetics for the committee to undertake the planning of the renovation of the upper church of Saint Aloysius. It was not until I was in my seventies that I began a more detailed research to document its history to share it with you. Much of the fading oral as well as the recorded information varies factually with its sources. I selected to write about those particulars of interest to me related to my profession in the world of fine art and the concerns of professional artists I have represented. If I am spreading any myths connected with St. Al's, I take the responsibility.

This book is about the ascent of Saint Aloysius Church (b.1859) and the recognition of its architecture and art. When I felt it was necessary to repeat information about certain aspects of the church's features, I did so to reemphasize their importance at that point in the narrative. I have not said much about the history of the parish itself but to focus on the values of this landmark structure in the city of Washington since the mid-eighteen hundreds. The history of the parish is being recorded by a much more knowledgeable author.

It is the great spiritual experience of those who can see invisible things what is to be learned and realized in that which is visible. The structure is striking but its deeper beauty is in the back story and admirable efforts the church's creators reveal in this historical and spiritual landmark.

The ground I chose to occupy contains some history, visuals and reflections about the building of St. Al's on North Capitol Street in the Federal City of Washington starting in eighteen fifty-seven. I feel this book has been needed to accompany the wedding ceremonies and events conducted here. Many will enjoy this book as a reference to the church's style and the art found within it walls.

My task was to call attention and add aesthetic plus a spiritual element of sense to the creation of specific pieces of art and architecture. I find the art to be honest and expressive created with the beauty that flows from genius motivated by a faith. Where this expressed genius stops pertaining to religion, it never stops being poetry itself. I consider the art a poetic expression. The art and architecture saturate the entire space for the greater glory of God.

Recall that the artists and architect of this place emigrated from Italy to plant a seed and way of giving a Jesuit presence in a growing America. Saint Aloysius Church rose up strong in a City where the past and present were severely tested. Saint Aloysius still stands fit and tall. No doubt more challenges to its survival will present themselves in the future.

Bob Murray, Author

Robert F. Murray, Author & Gallerist

A Lily in a Swamp

This sacred city place has flowered to a fragrance of greatness.
It generates from outside the earth,
It grows from a descending seed, a shoot,
Sprouting a stronger stem.

Planted in a barren, damp and troubled spot.
It was to become firmly rooted
In the small plot of an inner city of Early America.

This architectural flower flourished
In the center bed of a foundation,
Growing in personal, civil, national and spiritual freedoms.

Nourished by the visions of souls
Who put beauty and purpose
Into its remarkable form.

This dynamic space thrived to what stands, vertically,
As a prominent centerpiece
In a once upon a time swamp, once an unpleasant spot

In sight of the Nation's Capitol Building.

Rooting in spite of national stress,
Symbolic Lilies appeared, encircling its marbled sanctuary.

Solid, upright and serene, it stood
A focal point in the Hill's eye view
Of North Capitol Street.

xxii

Detail Vestibule Mural

Main altar painting by Constantino Brumidi

Centered in the sanctuary
And imposing,
A Master's huge canvas, significantly placed,
Showing a 16th century young boy, kneeling,
Well born, vowed and eventually professed
To later become chosen as a symbol
For the Glory, the Integrity, Stability and Dignity of Youth.

Aloysius Gonzaga, his spirit still intact
Like the Lilies,
Goes untouched by the ages,
At this hybrid church junction of Washington, D.C.

1

Planted in Uncertain Soil

BREAKING NEWS

In April 2017, all major media channels in the Metropolitan Washington, D.C. Area broke into regular broadcasts saying that early afternoon sudden sheer windblasts had severely damaged the roof of the Lily of Swampoodle, the Jesuit Church of Saint Aloysius Gonzaga. This incident was a startling reminder of the importance of this church structure landmark to the City. Franklin Duane, the former overseeing architect of the 1994 Saint Aloysius Renovation stated at that time that it is probably the original architect's use of 10' California redwood beams that supported the interior ceiling from collapse and from more devastating damage to the church. Just how these beams came to be transported from California to the Federal City of 1859 as well as their actual source, remains a question of interest.

Repairs Begin

The Lily, St. Aloysius Church, 900 North Capitol St. N.W. Washington, D.C.

The Church of Saint Aloysius Gonzaga is over 150 years old, and its time spans from the restless days prior to the American Civil War to the present-day turbulence in the Middle East. In the mid 1800's the church had only glimpses of real stability as a new parish, but it always has been viewed (and so documented) as an historical monument in the City of Washington and in America. It so happened that the church building was dedicated on the same day, October 16, 1859, that Washington's home, Mount Vernon, became a National Monument. The same day dawned to witness John Brown's provocative raid on Harpers Ferry.

The city of Washington and the nation had experienced spurts of growing pains described as complex. "Swampoodle," the name given to the rural part of the City where Saint Aloysius was to build, was to lose, eventually, its damp, swampy reputation in the yearling years as the demographics of the City brought integrity to the later days of the 19th century and the early 20th. As the City, unexpectedly, expanded towards the western boundaries, the neighborhood surrounding all sides of the new Capitol Building took on a conflictive posture of prestige and poverty. Saint Aloysius Church was planted firmly with the foresight of the Jesuits. They established the place as a symbol of the Ignatian idea to be associated with the Inner City where thought and current topics of domestic and international interest stirred about and flowed freely to the minds of all.

Churches, like Saint Aloysius, treated as monuments and not maintained or kept from deterioration, wither along with their nearby surroundings. This often creates a situation that excludes new and practical uses for them. Like grand homes and rock-solid buildings built by superb craftsman, these edifices become, at the most, curious tourist destinations. The problem is these become symbols of a past; these places become frozen or pressed into a fading dried flower arrangement of mild attraction.

My intention here is to speak and look at the building, the structure and discuss Benedict Sestini, S.J., the Architect and his intentions concerning his selection of style and the art within. To do so, I presume the type of education that can speak to the art and the history and times it reflects. My own sense of obligation to this sacred place requires me to seek permission, not simply from the Jesuits who built and own the property, but due to my intensive role in the planning and oversight of the working committees for the 1991-1994 Renovation, I am required to have the consent of the structure itself, its artists and their art. I look to the proper future of the place and to an audience that will use and see it for its intended use. How goes the Jesuits, the City and the Nation, goes the future of Saint Aloysius Church. What of the Lily planted in a swamp, "Swampoodle?" Will it always stand, flourish or wilt away by the winds of other interests?

Since 1994, the Upper Church in the building is regarded as a brighter venue for traditional liturgies, concerts and other appropriate gatherings. This is the result of the renovation that successfully projected a landmark church, and the forming of the basic ingredients or intentions to "wake up" the place.

The church is still in need of upgrades while still holding its own stately position in the Inner-City neighborhoods that hold historic structures like the U.S. Capitol, the Supreme Court, the Library of Congress and their surroundings. The communities living in the adjoining streets are challenged by the continued presence of some of the City's poorest housing and harassed by "drug holes" and the homeless looking for some night shelter. The great complex of the Union Station, a few blocks for Saint Aloysius Church, has created a beehive of daily workers and commuters coming and going under the sounds of many church bells, constant resonance of traffic, soothing splashes of water fountains and flocks of homing pigeons – it is the City. Among the marbles and granites in the parks, people pass without knowing the meanings of the history around them.

Saint Aloysius is not the only historic church on Capitol Hill. All the other churches also reveal the taste and sensitivity of their builders when the City's culture was growing. None of the other churches have the unique treasured, gifted paintings by Constantine Brumidi, the painter of the Capitol for twenty-five years. No other monumental church was built in the same era, for the same purposes to fulfill an ideal that would support those in a time of the City and the Nation were threatened by a terrible Civil War and waged to question, topple and change the values of a system in trouble.

Early Washington

First Steps to Saint Al's

One early September day in 1949, for the first time, I trooped into Saint Aloysius Church with my new Gonzaga freshmen classmates. Most of us who are living are still well known to one another today, and we all have gathered for our '53 class reunions in the same places where we awed, at first glance, this stunning structure. I often still hear murmurs from the pews of our reactions then and from the spirits embodied in those thousands of men and women who also sat there for over 150 years, holding in their hearts the marvels seen but unexplained that contribute to the meaningfulness and history of this sacred place.

Preview

Looking for some quiet place to think, to rest? Saint Aloysius is a good option. So many overly decorated and ornamental church places are noisy. I know it is not usual to think of art and architecture in terms of sound, but it is worth giving it some thought. Often there is too much imagery with an overload of ideas and incidents behind it. There is architecture that is noisy and complicated. It is all too overdesigned to be considered as a prayerful, reflective setting.

A church structure like St. Aloysius Gonzaga and the art within it are relatively simple and quiet – suggesting levels of silence looked for consciously or subconsciously. The simplicity and clean lines of the outside structure are non-intrusive to observe. The symbolism behind the recognizable art within holds both a rich cultural history and enduring spiritual values of the present and remarkable past belonging to this place plus the reasons it was designed and constructed.

It is not necessary to know or understand all that has contributed to the century and one-half existence of this church. Grand and ordinary events

The Romanesque Façade

happened here. Political and spiritual leaders have been here. Many have come to celebrate or to meditate quietly. Jesuit College and University alumni know this place well.

The Start of Building
The Distant Past and Rise of Church Architecture

Early man, the hunter, came down from the mountains to plains and river valleys. He became the farmer and had to think of ways to shelter himself and his animals. As he looked around for available materials, he found reeds to plant upright into the ground and covered the frames with a pa-pyrus. He also used animal skins for cover and used rocks to make walls for protection. Fallen branches and bark were found as cover---somehow, someway he figured out a way and necessity to be protected from the cold. Man had begun to make a home.

Although man instinctively knew how to construct shelter he was not alone for   in the world the bees, the ants, the bears and birds were all also busily making shelter for themselves.

It was a long evolutionary process that eventually produced the early art medium of 'architecture.' Man had to learn the art of using materials before he could master the art of engineering and building. An attempt to trace the path from the days of building mud huts to the time of the pyramids and Greek and Roman temples would be a huge and frustrating experi-ence. Yet it is understandable how the primitive sacrificial place evolved into a Byzantine palace in the East and into the Romanesque monastery in the West; also, how the Gothic cathedral evolved from both the Byzantine and Romanesque structures. A bit slower to improve were the homes of mud huts that became several rooms instead of one and how that took thousands of years to become the cottages, houses and office complexes we have today. It appears that places of worship took on more of a speed in architecture, faster than the dwelling places of man.

People, overall, possess a spiritual relationship with buildings. A place to come away from normal life inherent in man; he needed a safe place to go to think, to pray to reflect. When architecture finally materialized, it enlarged and embellished the ideas, the thoughts and plans of groups of people. Architecture required and found large groups of people who organized their ways into civilizations that are the real ingredients for architecture to flourish. Architecture is a reasonable measure for the existence of civiliza-tion. It fortifies, as other products of society do not, that society strives to survive and progress beyond its present state. Architecture, in addition, is a cultural phenomenon that exposes data about a society that managed to create it with little prior information. Architecture significantly directs the main source of intelligent power in a civilization and it depicts what the major cultural concerns of that society were.
(See Appendix 1)

Doric Style Capital Meets Frieze Above Entry to Sacristy,
by James Sanders

Mural Detail. "St. Aloysius Church in Background," by Armen Kankanian

2

Seeded with Spirit and Integrity

Mine has been over a half century of concern. A half of that is about the survival of the building itself, and that of the great impact it had on the growth of architecture in the nineteenth century. This was the same era that the Capitol Building was being constructed and near completion prior to the American Civil War of 1861. The building is the Church of Saint Aloysius Gonzaga, 900 North Capitol Street N.W., Washington, D.C. designed by the Italian immigrant Jesuit priest, Benedict Sestini, S.J.

My more recent growing concerns arose from the apparent lack of understanding, recognition and appreciation for the nature of the architecture itself and for the meaning of the art in the interior of the church. Since I saw the church for the first time in September of 1949, when I entered Gonzaga College High School, I have been imbedded by the definite uniqueness of the place and its effect and motivating force on my artistic nature and my life.

A lasting impression deepened when given the wonderful opportunity to be a planning and working member of the Renovation Committee from 1991 to 1994. In those working years, I realized how little I had known about the art and architecture we were attempting to bring further into contemporary use and understanding.

Watercolor Working Sketch by Murray

The very first overwhelming sight is the great oil painting by Constantino Brumidi, the renowned artist of the U.S. Capitol, centered over the main altar. It is large, colorful and portrays an interior and solemn scene with figures of 16th century European nobility and wealth. The central kneeling figure is a young boy receiving communion from a prelate, who is richly vested in church attire. The surroundings show a formal gathering in an ornate gothic chapel setting. The boy appears to be making an intent connection, a reaching to take in what is being offered to him. It is a lot to comprehend at one glance, and it speaks to some important and an intimate moment that the artist was attempting to capture.

Now, at age 83 and as a tribal elder in the world of fine art, I have heard visitors and frequent church-goers express some wonderment over the meaning and impression of this painting. There is no sign that suggests a

Looking Over Main Altar into Nave, by James Sanders

title or the artist of this great work. In fact, there is only, from time to time, out of the good graces of a person involved in a church event, to provide any substantive information about this entire place. It just exists in the middle of Washington in a district of the City where there is not much stimulation to inquire about this building. It is simply another church building of some denomination. All manners of resident and working city folk go by without a glance or thoughts of where this building came from or what is inside. It is hidden within structure and its art meaning and a history that significantly affected life in Washington throughout its 150 years. Like much public art, its significance is invisible to most passersby.

There were times after construction in 1859 that Saint Aloysius played dominant roles as the City of Washington grew in its architecture and in its role in charting the map for the demographics that developed towards the western regions of the City. The City grew towards Georgetown leaving the North Capitol Street neighborhood to struggle with a declining residential population into a decidedly poor and commercial district. The post- Civil War 1800's, the complicated early 1900's with increasing poverty, wars and racial riots and then a more positive break to posterity at the end of the 1900's into the 2000's left their marks. In all these times, it stood at the bottom of "the Hill" in the inner city where the Jesuits had taken a stand as influentially and as long as they could. The lily, Saint Aloysius Church, was planted and growing.

Henry David Thoreau once said, "None are so old as they who have outlived enthusiasm." The word enthusiasm itself drives its meaning from the Greek, "en theos." It implies the arrival of some greater spirit to a situation. It is in me to focus attention to what anyone might first recognize on entering Saint Aloysius --- the fifteen by 11 foot oil canvas, "Aloysius Gonzaga Receiving the Eucharist from Archbishop Borromeo, Bishop of Milan." This masterpiece was painted in Washington by Constantino Brumidi and given as a gift in 1859 through the architect of the Church, Benedict Sestini, S.J. to the Jesuits. It remained in place affixed to a wood stretcher until the fall of 1993 when it was removed by Arthur Page, a noted Washington fine art conservator, for cleaning, painting, and repairs. It was again stretched affixed onto an aluminum-surfaced backing and returned for the reopening of the church in October 1994 upon completion of the renovation. The original wood stretcher was used intact under the newly restored painting and remains there now.

Detail Main Altar Painting

Although it is generally known that this composition was not an entirely original concept to Brumidi, it is invaluable artwork as a representation of Aloysius (Luis) Gonzaga, the selected patron of the church and of a spiritual happening that depicts the very core of Christianity – the Eucharist. It is obvious too that the setting was one of privilege and wealth, somewhat of a contrast to the environment and early parishioners in pre- Civil War Swampoodle. A closer look at the bottom of the painting reveals a single lily resting on the steps leading up to the altar. Sestini carried the "theme of the lily" throughout the interior architecture. I believe Sestini made his intentions known to his good friend, Brumidi, who worked the symbolic flower into four of his oil paintings in the church.

> There is a river that brings joy to the City of God,
> to the Sacred House of the Most High.
> God lives in the City,
> And it will never be destroyed…
> *Psalm 46*

Lily Relief in Frieze, by James Sanders

St. Aloysius, Marble Statue in Vestibule

The Place to Plant

The construction of Saint Aloysius Church, 900 North Capitol Street Northwest, Washington, D.C., was completed by the fall of 1859. Its dedication on October 16 happened on the same day that George Washington's Mount Vernon Estate became a National Treasure. It was also on the day that witnessed John Brown's Raid at Harpers Ferry. The American history of these pre-Civil War times was in its painful making. Race, creed, civil and national sentiments ran raw and rampant. It was into this climate and uncertain environment that the Jesuit Fathers of Georgetown College planted the seeds of their mission that they had begun to sow in the Federal City at the turn of the seventeenth century.

In 1806, the Jesuits were adopted into the Russian Province of the Society of Jesus. There appears to have always been a subtle Russian presence at Saint Aloysius made by the unique and historical experience of Empress Catherine of Russia, with the approval of Rome, making sovereign claim to the American Jesuits thereby escaping the Jesuits' suppression in 1776. This unexpected foreign action allowed the Jesuits to operate here until, by a decree of Pope Pius VII in 1814, the Society of Jesus was permitted to run their own organization in America and be canonically established.

To expand their ministry as Maryland Jesuits, an expansion necessitated the building of a new Church. The ideal location would have been in the central, northwest quadrant of the Capital, but the Jesuits were obliged to build in a very unsettled location, an almost unpopulated edge of the City known as "Swampoodle." A new Parish needed to be situated that extended on the East from Fifth Street, N.W. to the Anacostia River, and from Pennsylvania Avenue northerly to the Soldiers Home.

Swampoodle was a muddy, unrefined, barren section of the City even though it was just a few blocks from the rising Capitol Building. There was a two-story country house, the mansion of Sen. and Mrs. Douglas, on Birch's Hill situated on what is now First Street and facing toward New Jersey Avenue. Eye Street was insignificant at that time, and North Capitol Street was a country lane with open country to the East where there were picnic grounds and ball fields for children. In 1859 there was no residence for the Jesuit Fathers, so they had to commute from the Gonzaga School on F. Street N.W. for services in the church. When the structure was completed, steps led up to the rear door where the Sacristy was reached via a long dark hallway. The pastor at that time resided in the present south sacristy. The room above housed the sacristan. The assistant pastor lived in the other room above the north sacristy. These rooms in recent years are used, periodically, for needed various parish activities. These dated rooms are now in need of repair and were not included the most recent renovation scope of work.

Lily Planted in a Swamp, by James Sanders

Lily Planted in a Swamp

How could an immigrant Italian man to America be responsible for a church, in the mid 1800's, that became a landmark building in Washington, D.C.? No ordinary man. It took a man who was a Jesuit priest, a Georgetown University mathematics professor, an astronomer and an architect with a mission. That was the lot of Benedict Sestini, S. J., who found the initiative to design and create, in addition to a few other East Coast churches, The Church of Saint Aloysius Gonzaga, 900 North Capitol Street, Washington, D.C. (called the Federal City in 1859).

Sestini was a friend of another immigrant artist, Constantine Brumidi, a.k.a. the Artist (the Michelangelo) of the Capitol. As Brumidi pursued his 25-year commitment to decorative painting in the Capitol, he completed various other commissions that included many religious-themed works for churches. By his association with the Jesuits and Sestini, he donated five large canvases to Saint Aloysius. The jewel in the crown is the central altar painting of Aloysius (Luis) receiving the Eucharist from Archbishop Charles Borromeo, cousin to Aloysius, upon the occasion of his visit to the Gonzaga estate in the mid 1500's. Within this painting as well as within the decorative architectural elements of the building itself dwells the creative collaboration of the Architect and the Artist.

The architectural style and its derivation is a big part of the Church's story. It was in an area of the City that, at that time, was a wet mess and swampy all around and up to the Capitol under construction on "the Hill" a mile away. Why and how did it manage to survive through a Civil War about to spill into the streets? Unpredictable changing demographics of the City, economic depressions, other war times, and recent civil riotous times and changes, all contribute to the developing drama of the stability of this place. Question is how will it weather the future?

This 'place,' this uniquely Washington landmark, is a place of reprieve for the soul. It has survived the rigors time, civil, political and religious personalities and the wavering elements of nature. This place has undergone minor and more major renovations through its 150 years that have made the structure endure as a dignified, stable and recognizable monument in the current environment of the City, the Nation and the World.

Benedict Sestini, who can be seen in the Brumidi altarpiece painting, would be a welcomed celebrity today if he could be here to say more about the plan and intention for the design and its integrity. From the front porch he would see students, politicians, businessmen, street folk and a very integrated representation of city life passing by; on occasion one or two running in and out of the church for a brief pause. He would fit himself naturally into the fabric of this church neighborhood, this place that he sank down deep into the City's soil. Perhaps he would realize how he filled an empty silence in our modern world. His church still arises from the depths of its inmost artistic personality – a statement, a prayer, a poem, maybe even a song that sings out over Union Station and the Capitol itself.

For me, once its student, its lifetime alumnus, a contributing renovator, Saint Aloysius Church stands as a metaphor to its patron, Aloysius Gonzaga, symbolizing a fresh wave of love and flowing through all human activities. This place stands strongly rooted as an architectural work of art and the spirit to every truth.

The Fabled Tiber River
Running Through the Early City of Washington

There was water that visibly meandered from north to south near the church of Saint Aloysius. Now and in the 1800's it never ran under or dangerously near the St. Aloysius Church property as many have misunderstood. It was what we came to know as the storied "Tiber Creek." Where, really, did this Creek flow?

It is of environmental interest to know and position the Tiber at the time of the building of the church. It helps to realize what a strange decision or choice it was to select a wet area of the City's boundaries to place a new church of size and prominence. *Life on the Potomac River*, by Edwin Beitzell, presents a section, Recollections of the Southwest Washington Waterfront, by Caroline Wimsatt that presents a picture of Washington in the mid 1800's. She writes how her father described the harsh winters in the City near the Potomac River when the docks were so thick with ice that the constant river traffic came to a halt. She said the channel of the Potomac was thick with silt and the River froze over so well that people ice-skated to Alexandria and back.

Early 19th Century Washington

In *Recollections* she wrote:

> that when she was a girl living on Seventh Street, it was called
> the Long Pavement and it ran from the Market House to B Street
> South." She recorded that there was a canal (Tiber Creek) where B
> Street North was about the time of the Civil War. This canal sepa-
> rated the southern part of the City from the northern part, connect-
> ing with the Potomac River at one end, and with the Eastern Branch
> at the other, making one island of south Washington. Even after the
> canal (Tiber) was covered, for many years this southern part of the
> City was known as the "Island." At the foot of Seventh Street was
> the wharf, the landing place for the riverboats; many carriages and

omnibuses passed before her home every day carrying passengers to the steamboats, one of which ran to Mount Vernon.

Earlier in Beitzell's book he pinpoints Goose Creek or Tiber Creek about a half mile below a Lear's Wharf; this creek flowed through the tidal flats, approximately near "B" Street, N.W. which is now Constitution Ave. Thomas Pope, one of the earlier landowners in this area, in 1663 had named his holdings that bordered on Goose Creek---"Rome." Even at this earlier time Goose Creek is called the TIBER in the deed, but as late as the 1800's both names were in use. It is evident that the Tiber flowed into the Bay called Goose Bay because of the great number of geese that fed there. Above the marshy estuary rose the sandstone Executive Mansion, flanked on one side by the brick Treasury building and on the other side by the partly built State and War Department building. In the early 1800's the Mall, a cow pasture in sight of the Washington Monument, was named "The Island." The Tiber separated it from the City.

As time went on, the Tiber connected two canals that ran to the Eastern Branch (Anacostia River) that opened navigation as early as 1816. Huge amounts of wood and produce were transported there in schooners, sloops and longboats. However, the accumulation of residues and waste turned the Tiber into an open sewer that generated the need to close it by covering it over in the 1870's, a decade after the building of Saint Aloysius Church.

Notable and related to the closing of the Tiber are references of the "Tidal Basin," once called "Tiber Bay" at the mouth of Tiber Creek. It was renamed "Tiber Bay" in 1802 by local real estate operators who had hoped to have the Federal City exceed in grandeur that of ancient Rome, on the Tiber River in Italy. Sailing ships, delivering the stone that we now observe in the bottom portions of the Washington Monument, moored their vessels in Tiber Bay. Renamed again, "Tidal Basin," by the U.S. Engineers, this body of meandering water was poorly engineered with the intention of having the tidal currents flush the Washington Channel of pollution and debris from the commercial markets on its banks. Once again, the ill-fated Tiber lost its proper use and fit into the architectural plans and the surrounding landscape of Washington.

The river's situations of the early Washington days spawned a cynical piece of poetry. The following verse was composed by a pro-British Irish poet,

Thomas Moore, who was not fond of Thomas Jefferson when he visited the White House in 1804.

> In fancy now, beneath the twilight gloom,
> Come, let me lead thee o'er this second Rome,
> Where tribunes rule, where dusky Davi bow,
> And what was Goose Creek once, is Tiber now.
> This embryo capital, where Fancy sees
> Squares in morasses, obelisks in trees;
> Which second-sighted seers, ev'n now adorn
> With shrines unbuilt and heroes yet unborn, though naught but woods
> And Jefferson they see,
> Where streets should run and sages 'ought' to be.
>
> Even now beside the Grand Potomac's streams,
> The medley mass of pride and misery
> Of whips and charters, manacles and rights
> Of slaving blacks and democratic whites.

These references help set the scene of the Federal City as it merged into the 19th century.

Earlier in 1789, nearby, on the heights of Georgetown, the Jesuits had established their college. Then, the view of the Potomac from the Healy Building's Tower Clock was a magnificent panorama that surpassed the sight from the Capitol Building. No doubt the bare land where Saint Aloysius Church was to rise in five decades was a continuing span of ground and growth. This view caused one of Georgetown's students to write:

"Beautiful River, bold and free,
Thy waters glide, how gracefully,
Queen mids't waters, 'tis to thee
I give the crown of sovereignty."

The years of history for both Gonzaga in the City and Georgetown College coincide. The people of the City and the students, faculty and alumni of the College have always been close in wars and in peace times. What has influenced changes in the Citys' role in civic, national and government affairs has likewise moved the Jesuits to new levels of their commitment to the Ignatian ministry.

Firmly Rooted

Father Burchard Villager, S.J., took the task of building St. Aloysius Church. To his credit, also came other Jesuit Churches of very similar style; St. Ignatius in Baltimore, St. Ignatius in San Francisco and in a grander scale, the Church of the Gesu in Philadelphia. The ground on which the Church and later, the Rectory and St. Aloysius Gonzaga College was built, had been donated to the Jesuits by Ambrose Lynch, father of Father Ambrose Lynch, S.J. In consort with the architect, Benedict Sestini, S.J., the plans were completed on May 11, 1857, and the ground was broken in early June when the actual work began. Sestini was a Florentine Jesuit who had come to Georgetown College as the Professor of Natural Sciences. His plans for the design of the architecture have yet to be seen again, but from the history of Jesuit architecture in Europe, there are valid and reasonable assumptions to be made concerning his approach to a Jesuit Church in an inner city in America. The architecture speaks volumes for itself, although it would be wonderful to discover his own letters of intention or his actual drawings. The archival search goes on.

To complete the total architectural and artful décor inside the Church, Sestini called upon his good friend Constantino Brumidi who already had begun his own epoch twenty-five-year painting triumph as the "Michelangelo of the Capitol," creating paintings, frescos and interior décor seen by millions today. The five Brumidi oil paintings contributed to St. Aloysius Church reveal a story all its own about the history of liturgical art and the relationship to this Church and the selection of Saint Aloysius Gonzaga as the patron of the building.

Portraits of Aloysius Gonzaga

We have several artful likenesses of Aloysius Gonzaga throughout the Church and in the Gonzaga Complex on Eye Street. Brumidi painted his likeness into his three canvases. The largest artistic rendering is the marble sculpture at the Church's Entrance. For many years, the Jesuit Community held a small white marble bust of Aloysius that still holds a place of honor near the dining room. On the second level of the Jesuit Community Residence Aloysius is depicted in a large print of an oil painting showing him as a young man of privilege and rank close to the time when he entered the Society of Jesus.

All these works of art bear the comparable resemblances of this 16th century youth. This brings us to believe that we have a good idea or impression of how the living Aloysius appeared. Note here that Brumidi used a Gonzaga student, Albert Brooks at that time, for his model to complete the altar painting. Not much is known about this young student or why Brumidi selected him as a likeness to Aloysius Gonzaga.

We do know that Aloysius was rumored to be very appealing in looks with a slightly retiring personality. His remarkable persistence, against the

wishes of his prominent father, to take on a life of service and contemplation in the Jesuits, made Aloysius the consideration as an example of a young man who follows his own dream. Over and above the privileged life his family offered him, he went on to a simple life devoted to others. We know that at 23, he died as result of his hands-on work with victims of the Plague when he was carrying out his work as a Novice in his Jesuit formative years.

Aloysius was reported to have acquired an overly modest demeanor and subdued way of carrying himself when he entered the Jesuits. So much so to the concern of his early superiors, that he was ordered to wear a type of stiffer collar that would make him hold his head up straighter. Many representations of him in art show him in a ruffled collar, traditional attire for his time and rank. It seems that Aloysius gave up one manner of a collar for another. Both would be challenging to wear responsibly today.

St. Aloysius Gonzaga, Portrait from Life

Sanctuary Within the Praesidium Arch

In the center of the Baldachino at the uppermost part of Brumidi's altar canvas flies the Gonzaga Family coat of arms. The coat of arms is displayed in a fine circular mosaic of a large and colorful inset to the marble floor of the sanctuary. These efforts suggest to us the importance of his social rank at the time Aloysius dawned his new role and symbol in the Society of Jesus. This Jesuit symbol is centered at the top of the overreaching Praesidium arch separating the sanctuary from the nave.

Aloysius (Luis) Gonzaga, by Nathan Leibowitz

Apse Décor.

The Saint Aloysius Church
(in the style of Anthony de Mello, S. J.)

In the middle of the City
Stands a temple of an enduring, struggling belief system.
I gaze at this sacred place
And fantasize as I meditate.
I see the City where this temple stands.
Who built this place, for what purpose?
I envision the plans. I look for them,
For the architect, the builders, the carvers of the altar stone.
I search for the sources from where the art and the marble were acquired.
I wonder from where the money flowed
To undertake it all.
I conjure the thoughts and feelings of the builders

And of the congregation
When the structure rose from the Federal urban mud,
I can imagine I am there the day the church opened
As I actually was present that October Day in 1994
As the choral lauds rang clear to the Capitol.
The life of Saint Aloysius Gonzaga Church was renewed.
I see the candlelit procession, the oratorio, the choir,
The spiritual power in transfering the consecration.
I picture the awe on the faces and souls of all present….
...now past.
I know decades of peace this place has offered to many.
I cannot predict Saint Aloysius's future.
My meditation has turned to prayer in this confusion.

Sanctuary Angel

Watercolor by Murray

3

Rooted in Significance

Enter the Church

The appeal of openness as you enter Saint Aloysius Church is surprisingly wonderful. Eyes open widely to a reaching central aisle directed to the jewel-toned oil painting hanging over the main altar.

The entire space is a huge rectangle of light and openness unobstructed by standing pillars or sidewalls. The one huge room simply and modestly carries its purpose with carefully conceived paintings, a couple of statues – all surrounded by a tasteful choice of architectural decorative elements. The Lily, the flower of the Eucharist, appears but veiled in various forms throughout the wall arrangements and decoratively painted into the designs of the expansive vaulted ceiling. The primary colors in the geometric-patterned stained-glass windows bring a soft glow and tone to the neutral walls classically graced with fluted pilasters capped with the acanthus leaves in their Corinthian floral designs.

Nave, by James Sanders

Over main altar, Corinthian Style Capital

Above the slightly curved arch of the Baldachino over the main altar, Sesti-ni placed the circular, stained glass window of blue, yellow and burnt gold rays surrounding a central, wheat colored orb of glass suggestive of the focal point of the whole experience, the Eucharist. This sole architectural element gives notice to Sestini's own major contributions to the natural astrological sciences by his extraordinary work at Georgetown University; his pioneer work and efforts toward the study of sunspots in the solar system are well documented.

Two obviously prominent, enormous fluted-iron columns flank the main altar and support the Baldachino. This massive use of iron reminds us of the use of iron, widespread during those times, especially in the construction of the Capitol Dome, a heavy base iron core overlaid in marble.

The Swamp/Swampoodle, Aptly Named

It seemed like the edge of the City
That was to become the center of the world.
To build a monument on this land seemed foolish.
Sweet Heaven would send no miracle
To ease this hell.
Carelessness of men, the acts of nature
Allowed this place to stagnate and be bleak.

There were slippery streets that were never dry
And pocked with open sewers where rats came to starve.
Tattered paper and debris stood open to winds that beat the shacks of
all the blacks and whites, oddly mixed in awkward closeness to a newly
growing Federal City.

There was filth on the flimsy ceilings, dirt in the musty alley air.
Elbowed out of crowded wooden rooms, people were scattered all about
the alleys behind and back of mansions rising in brick and stone.
Every night the poor crouched in the cold on shabby benches, hovering
a never lifting stench; the heavy peopled and horse bred odors that rose
and sank in the mud, always the mud.

There were many acting out, painted girls on whose backs vulgar pictures
were tattooed; some in red, often on girls who were dead and luring men
no more. Lonesome children wandered around.

The regular folks, a little higher but somewhat safely away on the Hill,
were vague about these alleys and slums.
They quickly trotted by, eyes down or straight ahead. They needed these
folks to do their laundry, care for their horses, clean their homes.
Times were getting tougher before the Nation's War upon themselves.

This Nation's Capitol Building was beginning to show its renowned
silhouette. Lincoln was soon to bring his freeing spirit to Pennsylvania
Avenue. Real streets were emerging from old alleys and paths.

The proper ladies of the city were gliding about trying to keep their skirts
from dragging in the horse trodden mud. Life was getting better for some.

Sestini, Oil by Brumidi.

The American dream was under discussion in the halls of the politicians and merchants' entrepreneurs. They were getting city life all together and it was going to get bigger and more complex for the City's people to make a fantastic dream into a little bit of comfortable reality.

Ordinarily, in a growing city the third most important public edifice is a Cathedral; instead this City built the Treasury Building very close to the President's House. And way over to the north side, almost out of reach, Came to be a place of God in a damp "slum," a swamp, dubbed Swampoodle.

The familiar southern Washington rains fell in their usual fashioned way on the half-boiled, newly donated Jesuit piece of land on North Capitol Street that let out a rising roar of the Spirit and brought about an evening sun to glow on a church, a sacred place in the making. An unfamiliar new style of architecture for Washington, a simple, vertically solid and strong red brick edifice rose above the neighboring alleyways – the Church of Saint Aloysius Gonzaga by an Italian immigrant Jesuit priest and architect.

The stakes at hand offered new Hope to the City, the Nation and beyond.

Face to Face with Beneditto Sestini

The intricate graphite portrait of Benedict Sestini, S.J. by Nathan Leibowitz is more detailed than Brumidi's realistic oil depiction of Sestini in the main canvas in Saint Aloysius Church. Nathan's rendering and impression of Sestini is a more studied look into Sestini the man, the scientist, the mathematician folded into his priesthood and role as an architect.

As I sifted through Georgetown University's archival boxes about Sestini, I saw there was no passing up the notoriety and academic success his studies generated concerning our solar system, sun spots in particular. Sestini had really sidelined his former architectural life when he came to America and plunged into a memorable time as Professor of Natural Science. The Jesuits' recognition of his expertise in making specifications for a church structure and his design/drafting talents are revealed in his drawings for the construction and décor of Saint Aloysius Church among other significant churches on the East Coast of America. The entire manner of the man,

Sestini, brought me to wanting to understand more of the low-keyed personage who wove his talents and personal charisma together in the early planning days at Gonzaga in preparation to the ascent of the church in Swampoodle.

Here is one, very necessary characteristic in any artist that separates him from others. It is the ability to be truly imaginative and original. Also in the intuitive life of the spirit the imagination is put to important use as it expands the mind to understand as well as role play the principles and values in any undertaking that leads to a productive outcome. This is especially so for the architect because his "art medium is his architectural art." They are inseparable. An unimaginative, poorly conceived (or imagined) piece of architecture fails to carry good usage or longevity. I see that Benedict Sestini was uniquely complete in his own qualifications as the architect of a church structure dignified over time to become a national landmark. His other professional specialty in exploring heavens grounded his work of architectural art on earth.

Sestini was a man of letters. He was a master builder. In his formal Jesuit studies, he became a student of history, philosophy and theology. His curiosity and imagination pressed him into intense study of the universe, the sun and the stars in particular. Sestini lived up to the ideals expressed by Vituvius who, in more ancient times, composed the theoretical thesis of ancient Roman architecture that stated, "an architect should be a man of letters." Presumably, Sestini had excellent drafting skills for an architect of a structure like St. Aloysius Church and would have to be skilled enough in engineering techniques to make specifications for a contractor/builder to work in concert and follow his design plans. From Sestini's drawings came the senior contractor's detailed plans to build.

According to the Georgetown College Journal, Vol. 33, No.5, February 1905, an article "A Vignette From the Past," says, concerning Fr. Benedict Sestini, S.J., astronomer and mathematician at Georgetown College from 1849 to 1869, with the exception of six years, spent respectively in Frederick, MD, three years at Boston College, in Massachusetts and one year at Gonzaga College, Wash. D.C. He was a person of medium stature, clad in worn and antiquely fashioned raiment, carrying an ancient faded green umbrella. The simplicity of his appearance was suggestive of the charming cure outlined by Austin Dobson:

- BENEDICT   SESTINI -
· A R C H I T E C T ·
THE CHURCH OF
SAINT ALOYSIUS GONZAGA
900 NORT CAPITOL STREET N.W.
WASHINGTON, D.C.
ARTIST: NATHAN LEIBOWITZ 3·2012

> Monsieur the Cure down the street
> Comes with his kind old face,
> With his coat worn bare,
> And his straggling hair
> With his green umbrella case.

Father Sestini in his prime had a distinguished face which, combined with quiet dignity, had the depth of a profound scholar, the sweetness of an amiable man of God and the simplicity that goes for both. Brumidi included the good Father Sestini into the altar-piece canvas which he painted for the Saint Aloysius Church in Washington---a most appropriate commemoration---for *IT WAS ON PLANS DRAWN UP BY THE VENERABLE FATHER THAT CHURCH WAS CONSTRUCTED*. This statement is testimony to Sestini designing the church. Other of his drawings, letters of intention or plans are yet to be discovered. There is reference to some, one or two, of his framed drawings that once hung in the President's office at Gonzaga but are now missing. I suspect they are somewhere in the present Gonzaga Archives.

Farther down in that same *Georgetown College Journal* it states "…HE DREW UP THE PLANS FOR THE GEORGETOWN OBSERVATORY, HOLY TRINITY CHURCH, GEORGETOWN, ST. ALOYSIUS CHURCH AND WOODSTOCK COLLEGE, WOODSTOCK, MD." At Woodstock, also, he designed, with the help of Brother Mason, and painted on the ceiling of the library the entire solar system on a gigantic scale in a space, seventy by forty feet. The scheme of this fresco includes the central point of the Sun, the orbits of Jupiter, Saturn, Mercury, Venus, Neptune, the Earth and Mars, and the region of the Asteroids. Inside Saturn's orbit are portrayed the planets themselves on a scale of a magnitude proportional to that of the Sun, whose disk is represented by the orbit of Saturn. The planets are represented with their respective Encke's Comet, Biela's, Faye's, Halley's and Donati's of 1858; also, the comets of 1853, 1843 and 1744. Then there is the general celestial map, representing the Milky Way and all the stars visible to the naked eye. Elsewhere are represented Orion's Nebula (Herschel's observation), as well as some observed by the Earl of Ross. Finally, there are representations of the signs of the Zodiac, hemispheres of the globe, magnified sunspots and the solar sphere under the eclipse.

Photo by James Sanders

When you first see the ever-expanding, coffered ceiling of Saint Aloysius, you are struck by the imaginative use of repetitive form and the azure colors that sweep the span from front to back. The obvious deliberate intention to make such an open space topped by a celestial-like ceiling suggests a great architectural background and use of imagination. Not until 1993 did the color of blue appear on the ceiling for the former decors were decidedly subdued in gray-greens and in 1959 by a bad dosage of rose and teal colors, tipped with poor aluminum paint choice. The Renovation Committee selected colors, which are called, a Comfort Blue and a Cathedral Blue for the new décor. A substantial amount of gold leaf was applied for highlighting architectural details. Bob Thuman, in his attached letter appearing later in this text, talks about the "leafing." The Florentine Sestini at twenty years of age was the active assistant to Father Inghirami, the astronomer in charge of the great observatory founded by Cardinal Ximenes in Florence. When Sestini came to the Jesuits he studied under the renowned Andrea Carrafa, who distinguished himself as the famous professor of higher mathematics at the Roman College in the late 1840's. Add to that distinction Sestini's time with Fathers DeVico and Angelo Vecchi. When Sestini died, he was one of world's most noted astronomers and authorities on the physics of the sun.

Sestini's first contribution to science was a monograph on the color of the stars. At Georgetown in 1853, The United States Government published Sestini's study of the Sun's surface with engraved plates made from his drawings. At that time, it was considered the best work of the changes of the Sun's spots in the world. On July 29, 1858, Sestini oversaw the team of Jesuits who, in Denver Colorado, observed the total eclipse of the sun from which he made the sketch drawing of the Sun's corona during the period of the totality that became an invaluable contribution to the science of that phenomenon. In that same year he published "Principles of Cosmography," where in the introduction, he expressed the hope that his imperfect sketch might draw the student's attention to the magnificent and beautiful original which "cannot fail to excite feelings of admiration, love and gratitude towards its Author and the desire to one day see Him face to face."

Here at 900 North Capitol Street we come face to face with Sestini, the simple man, the astronomer, the mathematician, the scientist, the priest-architect. He presents us with his own version of a traditional-Italian-Renaissance-Romanesque church structure built on a marshy edge of the Federal

City of Washington, a.k.a., Swampoodle, when an American war crisis was about to strike.

Sestini, the man, the Jesuit, had more than a faded green umbrella and a wishful prayer to fashion a church. He had the engineering ability to master a plan for a fitting exterior with a useful interior. His vision had to take in certain considerations of functionality. He had to envision the proposed space or land area to form the object for the people who would see and use it. This new object would have an obligation to humanity. It would be observed as a structure in a space under the influence of the day's light, weather; it would make sense in this growing City.

The exteriors in architecture rise in a spot created by constructing a building, a manmade frame or container for a designated purpose. In some earlier culture, a space designated for religious purposes was often an open space with some boundaries but usually no roofing. It was often a rock, a bluff, a hill, a waterside, a wooded area – some spot restricted to solitude for prayer or rituals. Eventually man wanted a more secure, covered place with furnishings and artifacts compatible to their practices. In time, structures called temples or churches were demanded from those known as architects to create the places for the sunlight of the Spirit to enter.

The Earliest Known Photo of Interior (1867)

Enter the Spirit as it will, both the paintings and the architecture serve as tangible, physical symbols. Yet the structure of the building serves only as a physical function. Here is where the role of Sestini differs from that of Brumidi. The architecture of the physical church serves as the container for whatever it holds. This is a fine point and can better be explained by realizing both the building and the paintings and décor within it are objects to be "looked at" by the people who use them. The difference between a painting and a building is that, for instance, the Brumidi paintings are used by looking at them, while Sestini's building is not only to be observed but is seen "doing" something, performing in its purpose. Sestini had to handle the problems of function while Brumidi had to consider superficial beauty within the walls or the container. Their combined artistic roles are what makes St. Al's the continuing success it is as a comprehensive work of art.

Engaging Sestini, the Immigrant Architect Priest

Watercolor Sketch of Capital by Murray

Despite not being able to find actual blueprints or their equivalents, nor letters of intention for the design and building of the 1859 Saint Aloysius Church structure, I will draw my own assumptions of his knowledge, Jesuit thinking and approach to the architectural project he was requested to do.

Sestini would have known, at the time, that he would be the only Italian architect near the Federal City of Washington, with the combined role, "artist-architect-priest." His Jesuit superior's password was for Sestini to create a new church community in an inner-city location where a European, artistic architectural background in church design would be able to solve the needs of the American Jesuits with European-related artistic and religious gestures. He was aware that if he would work in tandem with the interior artist, Brumidi, anticipating their combination of historical thoughts in art, it would make them even more fully-fledged participants in producing a significant church structure unlike any other in the City. The calculations and design by Sestini coupled with the poetic and classical artistry by Brumidi would grip them both into a whirlpool of a beautiful unseen success for the Jesuits and, perhaps, for the future of public buildings (e.g., the Corcoran Gallery of Art) yet to come in the Federal City. Their imaginations interlaced with their technical expertise of techniques, fashioned an architectural masterpiece to rise out of an untidy marsh.

The Federal City of Washington was already a famous city in the 1850's. When Sestini first saw the City, it was relatively lacking in memorable public building architecture except for the White House and government related building in progress. He was aware of other churches or sacred places in the region but there were no great church structures. He saw the opportunity to design a practical but memorable structure that would transform an insignificant piece of inner city land, near the rising Capitol Hill. Other church buildings would soon follow, but the St. Aloysius Church structure would redefine a new section of the City. An unseen, uncomplicated, sturdy Renaissance/ Romanesque brickbuilding appeared – The Saint Aloysius Church on North Capitol Street flowered in Swampoodle.

This structure's spiritual and historical symbolism has presently become clouded in Washington's history. This structure now rises into sight when the morning turns to noon. Its imposing shape fades into a forest of looming building cranes peppering the surrounding city blocks. The famous bells in the clock tower do not ring often and when the day turns to night again, the tower is a silhouette shadowing the years gone by. A study of this building and its decor is a look into its cultural relationship to human behavior. It tells a story of Sestini, the priest-architect, in his professional and political relationship with the City, his fellow Jesuits and their work.

It was not only Sestini's inner relationship to his work but the manner of his professional techniques that engaged me.

Sestini was an artist as well as an architect when he came from Rome to Georgetown to take the seat as Professor of Natural Sciences. He became professionally- known for his extensive work and study of sunspots and for his illustrations of his findings. In his time, he also painted a ceiling mural of the solar system in the Jesuit Woodstock Theological College in Maryland which is no longer. Although an accomplished painter, he understood the musical condition in painting that comes spontaneously from within. As a Jesuit-educated religious, Sestini had a multidisciplinary sensitivity that meshed all art, architecture and archeology into human recognition. His visuals took on a rhythmic, melodic quality, i.e., an inner nature that contributes to visual transitions in the art; this inner sense is what puts the artist's mark into the work. In essence, Sestini's inner artistic sense did this – stone, brick, plaster and mortar were his pallet or keyboard. His strong, directed hands and eyes were his guided hammers. His soul directed his inner movements that made music of his architecture.

The harmony created out of his intuitive sensibilities ultimately jelled with Brumidi's painting genius. Both of their guiding artistic principles put Saint Aloysius Church in place. Could these accomplishments ever be lost to the neighborhood and the City.

Interior Stairwell

Churches Are Odd

They are places of the most serious, sublime and joyous happenings. Often, they are empty and silent with the singleness of purpose to be open when needed. Their doors are closed, and the lights are off much of the time. Mainly, a church is for praying and serving a place for connection to God. One could ask, do we need a building or a structure to contain our prayers.

The church structure is often a lonely place. It is difficult to comprehend how architects come to design church structures that frequently differ in style and setting. We wonder if they always suit their locations and their purposes in the first place. Church structures range from being minimal in concept, design and execution to being very elaborate and ornate. On "church" Sundays the areas for rituals are full but left almost empty the rest of the days. They are similar to spiritual stadiums lit up for the liturgy or service of the week. It would seem that praying could be a much more practical exercise done in a simpler setting. There must be some other purposes for building churches. Like Saint Aloysius Church in Washington, the church was built to make a statement of purpose and recognizable mission.

It is doubtful the Jesuit Architect, Benedict Sestini or the Artist of the Capitol, Constantino Brumidi, would have planned for Saint Aloysius Church without direct, meaningful reasons and coordinated objectives to combine the exterior design to the interior. Since they were personal and working friends, both being immigrants from Italy, they chose to collaborate on creating a church structure by incorporating symbols of the classical "lily" in different forms in the architecture and the paintings themselves. The lily signifies the ideal, fresh youthful character of Aloysius Gonzaga – conveyed for centuries as the ideal patron of Youth. Question arises - did both artists succeed in carrying out that message of the Saint in the structure itself enhanced by the art within it?

More on Sestini

Sestini, like all architects, knew that his church architecture was a process and not simply a product. Any consideration for the design without had to incorporate plans for the objects within. If farsighted, he would have given

Detail of lily, altar painting

thought to how or why the building would have to be improved at some time in the future. We do not know his awareness of the future. We can assume that Sestini had the spirit to look beyond and within the realm of the project's design and gave serious thought to the restrictions of the restricted size of the land on which the church would be built; he understood its necessity to be rather compact in design and to be affordable at that time.

The economic situation for the Jesuits in 1857 was as tight as it was for all at the time. We know that the Jesuits joined with enormous fund-raising efforts by the prospective parishioners in the building of St. Aloysius. The Jesuit Community ledgers record various amounts in school and parish loans to Fr. Sestini for the building project. If these loans were "totally paid back" is uncertain.

Of particular interest to the building project is how Sestini was involved or handled the zoning situation at the time. No other building in the area, except for the rising Capitol Building, suggested the necessity for such a grand-mannered project of a church structure to be constructed. Usually, in a growing city like Washington, there was great emphasis on the building of a cathedral type structure that would mark the City as a great new metropolis. Instead the government embarked on the construction of the Treasury building that still stands as a huge block on Pennsylvania Avenue, which flows from the Hill to the President's House. Yet, over in the lesser reaches of the City, up sprouted Saint Aloysius Church. It was a large unforeseen entry, not in the formal plan for the growing City. We here take into consideration the recent call for an end to the height limitations within the District of Columbia. Since it is the low-rise nature of the city that makes Washington a unique metropolis in the world today, we can only conjecture the reactions of those concerned in the Federal City's planning when they realized St. Al's happening in the neighborhood of the Capitol.

Basic Architectural Styles of the St. Aloysius Church Structure

There are specific, defined parts of this structure's architecture, that have a definite name. In Renaissance architecture like the Saint Aloysius Church structure, there are many slight deviations or nuances employed by the architects and builders to meld together certain elements of style into variations. For instance, there are elements of the Gothic that occur in that Romanesque that blend into parts of the Baroque, etc. etc. Usually the finished structure represents one certain style more than any other – as Saint Aloysius Church stands more as an example of Romanesque style than any other. It is decidedly Italian by the Italian Architect, Benedict Sestini, S.J.

As one approaches the front of the church, there are central steps at street level that split to the right and to the left at a landing and continue up to the porch surrounded by three-foot-high concrete columns with banister. The "façade" is the architectural, exterior front of the building. The façade of Saint Aloysius has a flight of steps and a central portico with three pediments over the entrance doors. Each door has a Tudor arch above it. The windows along both sides of the structure and the windows at the second and third levels of the façade have closed architraves. The roof style is one of a simple ridge or gabled roof. The clock tower to the right rear side of the structure has two horizontal divisions with a cornice, parapet and central feature housing the bells. The entire exterior is red brick with stucco accent at the window levels. To first appearance, the structure is Roman-

Praesidium Arch and Dome

esque---simple, plain with clean lines and relatively unimpressive. Inside, the eyes capture with the unexpected quiet an open grandeur. The ceiling, the cover of the inner roof, is a combination of flat and inset surfaces. It hovers over the nave, the central part of the interior. In Saint Aloysius, the ceiling is a repeating motive having twenty-six, ten-foot squares with outer beams or struts. The ceiling in the sanctuary displays a dome of coffered and paneled motif with an oval, central stained-glass window. The wall at the top back of the interior displays a rose window design of opaque opal glass. All the sections of glass appear supported by a series of diagonal ribbed vaults.

The original seating plan showed a central and two side aisles, serving a group with light from two sides and access at the corners. The original center aisle floor was slightly raised, leveling access into the pews. During the 1994 Renovation the seating was reconfigured to a grouping within a cruciform plan with central and side aisles allowing room for the new 26 foot extension of the main altar sanctuary platform. Also, all the aisles were made level at the time.

Jesuit Style

Gesù Exterior, Rome

Whether recognized or not, in the time of the nineteenth century, the Jesuits had been building for three centuries. Many examples of their monumental churches were in Munich, Paris, Vienna, Prague, Florence and Rome. All around the world the Jesuits had been putting up structures called 'Jesuit Structures or Style." For hundreds of years to the nineteenth century, the Jesuits were associated with baroque art, especially in Germany. Many churches were highly decorated with ornate images and paintings that made them stand apart and above other structures. The Jesuits were often accused of overly decorating their churches with emphasis on" pomp "as a manipulative measure within a church that professed poverty. Later, it was thought that when they began to build a simpler styled church in Italy, their buildings should appear somewhat less distinguishable from other city buildings. This did not seem to be fair criticism since Jesuit churches always had a particular character of their own about them. It is now obvious that the building of The Church of the Gesu in Rome set a "Jesuit" standard for architecture, reflected in variations around the world. There

Gesù Interior, Rome

would be an intention to have all Jesuit churches to come into the New World to be a reflection back to Rome. Saint Aloysius Church by Sestini's designs is a modest variation of the Gesu.

There probably is no such strict style known as Jesuit style. For after centuries of designing churches of ornate and baroque styles in architecture, the Jesuits, a religious order, embraced many different styles to suit their ministries at a given time. A hypothetical run through Europe, all the Americas and parts of Asia, the Jesuit style reveals contemporary trends in building churches and the ways in which the Jesuits appealed to all the senses in spreading their message. Ignatius Loyola urged the appeal to all the senses in understanding the existence of the reign of God. When man began to recognize that great symbols of a cultured people was found in their architecture, there was an enormous thrust of activity to create structures that carried the message of a cultivated society. As a result, and in many recognizable instances, church architecture far outstripped any real, detailed understanding of the theology the architecture represented. The results were pomp, but no spiritual circumstances to boast. It all seemed like a needless overkill of design, technical and manual superiority. The Jesuits, however, by the 18th century, evened out their attitudes about erecting churches for show and settled into a practical sense of building church structures that would be useful and contain recognizably and clearly depicted images (painting and sculpture) that would easily be viewed as carrying the stories and meaning of Christian spirituality. Although many Jesuit-built churches on the East Coast of America became simplified in decorative elements, they often still emerge or are criticized in our times as too elaborate and highly overworked for present liturgical purposes and tastes. Some now feel critical and rather unaffected by the glitz and materialistically opulent treatments in churches, cathedrals, basilicas and like religious structures. The younger generations seem to disregard the sights and visitations to such places as sacred as we did up to the mid-19th century. Godland and Disneyland seem to be an uninspiring mix. In fact, this sentiment is becoming more evident by the unfortunate actions of the Jesuits themselves in failing to maintain treasures of art that originally found their way into their churches. There are painful cases where valuable art has been tossed away to make way for a newer way to better portray a spirituality in a more contemporary mode. These losses and lack of cultural concerns remain talking points when new church constructions are in play. Church buildings dating from the 17th, 18th and 19th centuries disappeared almost overnight without much attention to what has been lost for good. What is left are a few concerned onlookers to investigate what could have occupied the vacated sacred space.

Jesuit Style

A few blocks walk or car ride down North Capitol Street from the Capitol a large, plain, red-brick-box-of-a-building appears on the left-hand side of the street.

It stands upright at the end of the large block of land that comprises the Gonzaga College High School at the other end of the complex with the Jesuit Residence in the center. The Church outside is not exactly as attractive as it is imposing. If the interior were painted entirely white, it would appear to be a large, white cube. The old Government Printing Office, a block away, has always been a more recognized Washington landmark. In more recent years, the façade of a neighboring large red brick building, commissioned and built to be the New District of Columbia Office Building, was designed to somewhat resemble the Church. Both buildings serve like bookends separated by the Gonzaga track and field. As large as the Church building is, it stands without much notice as people and cars pass by. There is little distinction in the decoration or style of the architecture that would attract special attention. Yet the building and style of this Jesuit Church set an architectural trend for architects and city planners in the City of Washington in the middle 1800's and to this day.

Capitol in Background

It is not absurd to think that over one hundred and fifty years ago, as the U.S. Capitol Building was nearing completion, that there was not some recognition of another very new bold structure causing attention and curiosity rising on North Capitol Street. Dr. William Thornton's design for the new Capitol selected in 1793 by George Washington, won the architectural competition in the Federal capital district. Under his supervision as Architect of the Capitol, Thornton pressed ahead to include in this classical architectural work the decorative sculpture work of Benjamin Latrobe and the significant paintings and décor of the Italian Immigrant, Constantino Brumidi. This is the same Brumidi who, at the same time, was working in the interior of Saint Aloysius. The frieze along the interior walls of the church was applied under his supervision by the same artisans who were doing decorative painting in the Capitol. Brumidi's close personal association with the Italian immigrant priest, Benedict Sestini S.J., architect of Saint Aloysius Church, would bring five paintings invaluable to the interior. Their shared work experience going on at that time must have gained more than casual attention to those particularly interested in the growth of the Federal City and to what kind of urban architectural path of design to follow. Doubtful as it may be, the thoughts of any "Jesuit Style or Design," could have resonated in the memories of those likened to the many churches of Europe, especially those in Italy. There must have been some professional notice of the rather stark kind of design this new place was taking on in an area of town reputed for its dirty, muddy streets and a rather bleak outlook at the time for any attractive residential growth or upward mobile society. Building a place like this church in a place like this seemed foolish.

Whatever the case is for the Jesuits themselves in caring or not affording to preserve the artwork and possible treasures they hold, the fact remains that a lot of art was discarded, poorly stored and not fitting the purposes of the Jesuits work at hand. Often, valuable art, donated to churches, schools and Jesuit residences, assumes anonymity of its own as years go by, but the memories and documentations of these gifts are not carefully registered, and their value gets lost for good. Those forgotten valuable works of art find themselves in attics and storerooms or to some general auctions of distribution. Some item of value and memory finds its way into the yard sales of the future to fit randomly into another generation's style or sense of value. We have in the instance of the architecture and art within the Church of Saint Aloysius the matter of "style," Jesuit style, and how or if it fits into this 21st century. Will the building be maintained to last for another 150 years or be replaced with another Jesuit need? Will the provenance of the art be properly kept for future reference?

So much is written and exhaustively explored discussing a "Jesuit Style." Most of what I have gathered comes from two books by contemporary Jesuits, Spirit, Style, Story, by John W. Padberg, S.J. and Landmarking, by Thomas M. Lucas, S.J. The term Jesuit Style is real and verified but I am choosing to change and refer "a style" to "a rhythm," — Jesuit Rhythm. Because for my purposes I sense a rather lyrical tendency of the Jesuits to make what they need and use for their work into an action that flows directly from their mission and purposes at hand. My sense from what I have observed of the architecture of Jesuit Churches, does not fall into one or two specific styles but projects several aspects of architecture styles and decorative, applied art onto a stage adaptable to the many events, performances and ceremonies needed in urban places of learning and liturgical functions. Jesuit places are places that sing to the music of the city. They planned their locations where city life and ideas flourish to retain the rhythm of contemporary thought and ideas. It is the Symphony of the Ignatian Way.

Lilies Detail in Vestibule Mural

Carrier of Lilies, by A. Kankanian

Composing His Masterpiece

When Brumidi was conceiving how he would approach the rendering of "Saint Aloysius Receiving Communion from Archbishop Borromeo," (this is the familiar title of the painting), he needed to discern how to make the painting relevant to the Federal City of Washington. We know that his completed composition of the painting was not a completely original concept of Brumidi's but was a direct adaptation of another work of an earlier artist. He needed to contemporize this traditional representation. His decision was to introduce portraits of real people known to the Washington community of the time. Whether it was last minute inspiration or a convenient afterthought, he dropped into a very central rather clever, less prominent noticeable spot in the composition, an impression of his own face – which is of a man appearing to be considerably older than he actually was in the 1850's.

The other living people that appear in the painting included Albert Brooks, a Gonzaga student at the time. He represented Saint Aloysius. Adele

Brumidi by Matthew Brady

Self-portrait, Brumidi, Main Altar Painting

The Jewel in the Crown

Douglas, second wife of Senator Douglas, depicted Aloysius' Mother. Father Sestini, S.J. is shown with hands folded on the right side of the canvas and the conjecture is that the priest with his back to viewers is Father Stonestreet, S.J., then the Jesuit Provincial or Father Villager, S.J., the Church Pastor. The father figure is thought to be Aloysius's brother, Rudolfo, and that Fr. Varsi's face may have been the model used to portray Archbishop Borromeo. Charles Borromeo, not incidentally, refashioned the seminaries in the sixteenth century. By choosing this representational ensemble of portraits, Brumidi covered his own personal and professional obligations to the City, the Jesuits and his own concepts of his work.

The architectural design in the Altar Painting's composition and its notoriety as extensive as it really is and in calculating the great percentage of the canvas's composition that the background consumes, it is no exaggeration to say that the finer details in the painting are somewhat lost --- especially since the viewing distance from the main center aisle is some 50 feet in

distance. The coloration of the Gonzaga home altar is an antique color of burnt gold pigment mixture in a heavy baroque style, much more elaborate than the architecture in Saint Aloysius Church.

The window arrangement in the center background is of gothic design origin. The vessels (implements used in the liturgies) on the altar are ornately turned metals and typical of renaissance liturgical artifacts used in the rituals or liturgies even today. The tall ornate candlestick holder is similar to many holders of the Paschal Candle used today.

What is recognizable is the contrast of the elaborate décor in the main painting in contrast to the architectural décor of the entire interior of

Detail Altar Painting

Saint Aloysius Church. For as many traditionally accepted classical decorative elements as there are in the interior, it appears Sestini used restraint in overly embellishing his work thereby making the church's future use more adaptable to changing times and styles.

The frame, known also as the surround, enclosing the main altar's canvas is built into the wall. It has not been changed or doctored since its installation in 1859. The construction of this frame is molded plaster that has an overlay of a silver pigment, overlaid with a wood-toned varnish. The frame appears to be of gold finish but is really the combination of silver leaf pigment and a wood-toned varnish that contributes to the total effect that complements the canvas itself.

The accompanying photos are part of the 1994 work-in-progress, daily, visual record of the return of the Brumidi paintings to the church after their restoration by Page Conservators, Washington, D.C. This event prompted The Washington Post to compliment the result of the Renovation. This led to the highest commendation for a church renovation of that year by the National Decorative Painters Association. In turn, Barbara Wolanin of the Office of the Architect of the Capitol of the U.S. made a presentation in St. Aloysius, to the many followers with her definitive book, published in 1994, about Constantino Brumidi's legacy for his 25 years of extraordinary, decorative painting in the Capitol. We need a similar praise concerning the life's work of Benedict Sestini, S.J. Architect.

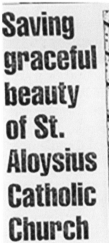 

Renovation Contractor, Ferrandi and Architect Duane

This is probably the best place to sight the use of the newly renovated, extended (26 feet) sanctuary's travertine marble floor for a formal piano recital performed by the Russian virtuoso, Youri Pochtar, in the first months after the Renovation. Upon invitation from a Gonzaga alumnus, Ashley Hawken (1953), Youri came from Paris, where he now resides, to give this special concert for us. Many photos of him against the background of Brumidi's masterpiece made worldwide publicity of the concert event. We are hoping, if the opportunity is right, that more concerts, musical recitals and appropriate events of this kind will continue in the future of the church.

Impressionistic Photo, Youri Pochtar (from Paris) in Concert

Lastingness, Brumidi's Claim to Youth

It would be difficult to define the altar painting as Brumidi's best work. Like most other of his oils, this canvas's composition is orderly, proportional and relates a story. His paintings appear realistic and recognized for the characters and scenarios he meant to depict. Brumidi went about his painting in a very orderly fashion. He was a student of classic and natu-

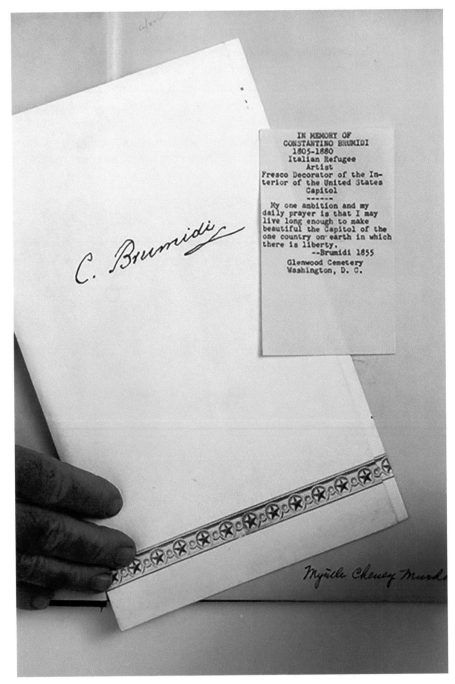

Brumidi's Signature and Note of Epitaph at Glenwood Cemetery, Washington, D.C.,
Photograph by Ryan P. Connell

ral beauty that he represented in a known, traditional manner of painting. What is amazing is the volume of paintings he produced in his twenty five years of work in the Capitol and outside of it. More amazing is the time and focus he devoted to this particular altar painting he donated particularly for Saint Aloysius Church. No doubt, his close affiliation with Benedict Sestini, S.J., gave rise to the particular application of meaningfulness he instilled into his work to give another historical message as legacy to this historical place.

Leonardo DaVinci's widely rumored code seems to bear credence when art historians attempt to extract from the Last Supper the artist's personal attitude and affiliations with selected figures in the painting. Encoding or inscribing (for a visual artist, painting is his brand of writing) a spiritual or historical moment in painting of a religious nature is no novelty. Brumidi, in his Aloysius painting, goes to some lengths to include mid-nineteenth century personalities into a sixteenth century historical setting. Why did he do this? Was this a request on the part of Sestini or the Jesuits at that time? Did he make this composition according to his own decisions to imbed contemporary meaning into the canvas that he presumed would last for many years? Was Brumidi attempting to instill in this large work his own hope for lastingness – a profound desire of all real artists in any field of human endeavor? Have people over the last 150+ years derived any message from this work other than it is of an imposing size and fine quality of painting? What is this painting's message? Is this an inspired or inspiring work of art? Could we say that Brumidi had any code or hidden implication of some personal stand he took on religious, political or spiritual matters?

The self portrait of an older Brumidi is deliberately positioned in the center of the canvas, right under the outstretched arm of Borromeo offering the host to Aloysius. Unlike DaVinci's self-portrait in the "Last Supper," where DaVinci positions himself at the end of the table with his back and head turned away from Christ and his followers, Brumidi stares approvingly and affectionately toward Aloysius. The Artist makes a strong statement for the ages to come that he himself is pleased with this particular painting commission at this energetic time in his early American life as a citizen, that he wished to put himself in admiration of Youth, the Jesuits, and the Church. I say "Youth" to emphasize that longing of the Artist to continue his own youth through this painting.

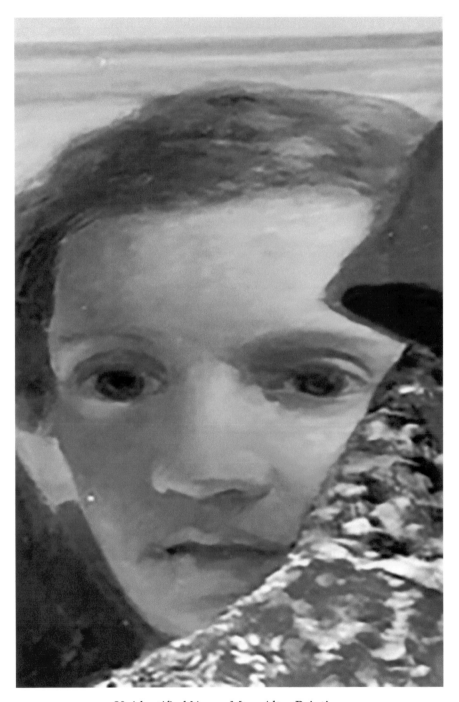

Unidentified Young Man, Altar Painting

Observing Adele Douglas

Observing the woman in the painting is key to its understanding. Brumidi personally knew Adele Douglas, second wife of the famed, "The Little Giant," Senator Stephen A. Douglas, from his many days working in the Capitol. Brumidi certainly would have been aware of the heated slavery issues and the related debates of 1858 and the vibrant presidential election of 1860 between her Douglas and Lincoln. By her marriage to Douglas, Adele had two step-sons at Gonzaga, Stephen Douglas and Robert Douglas. Her founding association with the beginnings of the College High School and its goals would have given Brumidi good and appropriate reason to have her pose for a portrait to be included in a portrayal of a young man about the same age as students at Gonzaga. The composition required a mature woman of integrity to act as the mother figure to young Aloysius Gonzaga. The setting was to be the home chapel of the Gonzaga family of means that would mark the unusual visitation of Aloysius's controversial uncle, Archbishop Borromeo of Milan, taking the opportunity to give Aloysius the Eucharist for his first time. What better fit model for Aloysius's mother than the benefactor, Adele Douglas who had offered her nearby home on New Jersey Ave. and generosity to the Jesuits at Gonzaga. It would be a few years later, when Mrs. Douglas would attempt a failed, last minute personal clemency appeal to President Johnson for Mrs. Surrat, hung for her questionable part in the death of Lincoln.

In Brumidi's portrayal of Adele Douglas, he strikes a familiar style of the Madonna-like position of a mother in a gaze of admiration for her son. She is seen as the proper, iconic woman in a customary lace headdress.

Brumidi painted many representations of the Madonna in churches and in private for many years in Italy and America. Many versions of women in his other paintings have all the same demeanor and similar appearance. In this work, Mrs. Douglas has many of her real characteristics, but her visage is somewhat idealized for this classic painting. Adele is recognized often in her photographs as a "beautiful woman" in her time.

Adele Douglas as Mother of Aloysius in Main Canvas

If it is possible to describe a major role in poetic prose, I will attempt it with the fol-lowing:

Breathing in the cool, clear October air of 1858, with brush in hand,
Constantino reaches upward to the 15-foot canvas, as if coming closer to heaven,
He moves patiently, elegantly to make place for her delicate features;
We see him moving in the creative process, carefully.
A woman of true iconic beauty is beginning to form,
A veil of intricate lace takes shape over a bowing head
As the Artist begins to add signs of soft colors of her complexion,
We are seeing signs of growing intense attitude of a mother's protective bond.

The colors are of her authoritative personality,
The blushed reds and ivories are young in their seasons, with lightness and Grace.
Her face will have many decades to mature in its washed- gold frame.
The Artist lightly tips and dabs in a jeweled head comb woven in white lace,
The whites and highlights of gold pigments appear more prominently
As this woman kneels leaning toward the solemn situation.
The reverend blacks of her dress, slightly marbled with lace
Make the muted grayed-oranges tints
Across her glowing face.

As he completes the remaining canvas,
Brumidi strives to lessen her obvious appeal
By affecting fading of tones into the role of the other figures into one grander Scene.
Aloysius, her young son in a blue cape of humanity, will begin to emerge,
Centered to her attention.

The dusts and lights of ongoing time may dull, a bit, the total canvas,
Brumidi will not despair of this;
He will ensure that all autumn-summer-spring colors
Are preserved intact
For as long as his masterpiece exists.

The Unidentified Father Figure

As far as we know, Brumidi did not use a familiar model or personage known at that time to paint Aloysius's father. But we have learned that the standing father-figure was meant to be a portrait of Aloysius's older brother, Rudolfo. We know of his prominent father from other literature and of his great expectations for Aloysius to take rightful claim to the Gonzaga family fortune. Looking closely into the face of Brumidi's representation of the father figure, I attempt to understand from his subdued stance the way he came to feel and be touched about his son.

On the day you were born I found my hope.
You captured all my expectations for an heir.
As your young life blended with mine,
I thought we would never part...until my death.

So much more than I had ever dreamed of,
You overwhelmed me with your rare persona.
Your attractiveness and clarity of mind
Made mine not want to be away from you.

My life and fortune were now worth having
As everything came to have meaning in and solely for you.
You became my full friend not only my son.

But as I now proceed somewhat empty in this life,
I see your soul has taken its own flight
In a life I can only barely imagine.
I observe you now vanishing from my grasps of gold,
Reaching far beyond what I have to offer.
I know without understanding that you are making me whole
In this monumental moment of realizing that creative urge of the spirit.
Father and Son have become one.

Portrait of Rudolfo, Older Brother of Aloysius.
Brumidi's Choice for Father Figure

Brumidi's Other Paintings in St. Al's

Brumidi's two tondos (round wall canvases, originally thought to have been planned as raised-relief works) representing events, related in the Saint Aloysius story, were removed for cleaning by Page Conservation. One depicts St. Margaret Mary Alocoque envisioning St. Aloysius in heaven. The matching tondo shows Aloysius kneeling before Mary and Child. The "Madonna" canvas and "The Two Trinities" canvas were treated by Armen Kankanian, after removal from the side altars. In the case of the larger, center altarpiece painting, it is known that Brumidi copied great master's paintings for adoption into church venues. "Master painters" by definition are recognized, trained copiers of other great works of art. We have always looked at the three main figures, Mary, Jesus, standing on a riser platform or stone, and Joseph situated in a background of the pyramids with an "Egyptian-like head relief" water source or wall fountain to the left on the canvas, usually called, "The Holy Family In Exile in Egypt." I learned that the correct title of this work is "The Two Trinities," originally by Murillo with a vertical composition of God the Father (upper part of canvas), the Holy Spirit (Dove), a little above the center of the canvas, and Jesus, (Son of God) elevated from the ground by the box or stone he is standing upon. Viewed horizontally, the artist's intention of the Christ as the central figure is apparent. Mary and Joseph complete the horizontal, threesome composition. Pyramids in the background suggest the Holy Family resided near Cairo, Egypt during the time of their diversion. There is speculation whether or not they went to Egypt and if it was an escape measure to obscure their actual whereabouts from Herod.

The associated cost of restoring this painting now by a Master Artist to its full complement would range into the six figures. Its actual worth would be determined by virtue of the history of its movement and of the Artist's notoriety. The monetary value of all art is contingent on many social, cultural, financial situations and art markets at any one time.

Watercolor Sketches #6 and #7 by Murray

Tondo Left of Praesidium Arch

Tondo Right of Praesidium Arch

Murray and Kankanian examining Brumidi paintings, 1993

Murray and Kankanian Examining Restored Painting

Illustration of Clock Tower by Nathan Leibowitz

Mortar to Brick, Brush to Canvas

Brick on brick up to the ten-foot, redwood ceiling beams, Benedict Sestini S.J., Architect, designed and built the Church of Saint Aloysius Gonzaga in the Federal City of Washington in 1859. His close friend, another Italian immigrant and Master Artist, Constantino Brumidi, joined with him in meaningfully decorating the Jesuit Church, a Romanesque-styled structure that would metaphorically reflect the characteristic virtues of its Patron, the young Jesuit, Saint Aloysius Gonzaga. Together they created a lasting landmark of and stability, dignity and integrity that still stands in the center of an ever-expanding City, a few blocks from the vortex of national and international power, the Capitol of the United States of America.

How well did Sestini meet the requirements for building and designing a city church? After previously reviewing and discussing many of the prominent elements in the interior and exterior of this structure without the advantages of discovering any of the Architect's actual letters of intention, preliminary plans or drawings, I felt prompted to find some contemporary and professional measures against which to judge his accomplishment. Sweeping through several books on church and public architecture, I found there were many schools of architecture, liturgical commissions and conferences and accomplished architects themselves whose environments and the availability of materials and labor, determined what could be built and where.

From the earliest Christian years, serious effort was expended to specify what would constitute the right kind of structure to take its stand as a community's sacred place of prayer. As times and circumstances changed, as the church populations grew and expanded their visions, architects met building standards and still had to maintain the practicality of creating a structure. Often, they went too far in overdesigning buildings that faded into periods of obsolescence. Too elaborate, too ornate, not enough space, inconvenient access, too much space to maintain, these were expressed frustrations....

Watercolor Sketch #5 by Murray

Of the many important liturgical conferences, one significant to our time came about in February 24-25, 1965 in Cleveland Ohio where 500 interested architects, clergy, artists, contractors' artists and members of liturgical and building commissions of America and Canada participated. Several related individuals presented papers on the subject of possible liturgical reforms. From these are extracted standing criteria against which to evaluate Sestini's nineteenth century design for an inner-city church structure. Did it then and does it now meet the purposes of its building?

Mosaic Detail in Altar Bench

City Structure in Background Designed to Complement the Church Architecture

The idea for practicality and thoughtful liturgical reform is usually to promote the need and creative genius that would shape the ritual act of the congregations as well as offer to architects and artists an atmosphere where they freely and profitably do their work. Understanding the liturgical values, the basic notions of worship for which a church structure is utilized, would be made clearer.

Without a doubt, I feel Sestini succeeded remarkably well given the turbulent times, the scarcity of funds and the marshy environmental conditions of the swampy region of the City. Considering exterior problems at hand and the interior design factors, the following pages are offered as my contemporary critique of St. Aloysius Church as a piece of architecture and of art.

Pope Francis, in his September 24, 2015 address to the U.S. Congress, repeatedly called for dialogue concerning these points in his address. "It follows that it will always be necessary for architects and artists to dialogue

about the uses, refinements and economics of their work. All involved in
the design and building of churches fitting to their locations and the uses
of their congregations will be reaching for the intangible... the perfectly inspired, designed, constructed and fitting structure for the use of its people,
invulnerable to all the elements of nature." Yet, 150+ years ago, Benedict
Sestini S.J. came up with a structure that has remained solid, and maintained a practical use in concert with its continual function. Consider the
attraction and stability of its exterior as well as the captivating appeal and
ongoing use of the interior.

The exterior design, basically, is Romanesque, a much-reduced version
of its famous predecessors the Church of St. Lorenzo in Florence and in
Rome, The Gesu. It fit and did not fit the place where situated. The structure suited the style of building beginning in the City, but it appeared too
grand for the Swampoodle neighborhood. The church structure blended
more into its setting when Gonzaga College came into its proximity and
the City grew and improved around it. Today it holds its own significance
as a worthwhile structure although being dwarfed by new constructions all
around it. For a church on a tight city plat, Sestini planned for the structure
that would utilize to the maximum its designated modest design reflecting
Jesuit practicality. He used brick, wood, mortar, plaster and cement – all
materials that endured for over a century. Only the bricks themselves become compromised in the early '30's when they were erroneously painted
for decorative purpose, weakening the brick's resistance to the elements
when the paint was improperly removed. Recently, with a new treatment,
this deterioration has ceased.

Today's new challenge for architects, as it was for Sestini in the mid-nineteenth century, is to make an interior setting that requires a whole new
psychological space. The older, piously-subdued lighting effect is out. The
space has to fit community action. Sestini conformed to these directives by
designing an open space, bright with large windows (initially, were clear
glass) although the interior being limited originally to the low night light
of gas lighting. Since the earlier Jesuit architecture was criticized as too
elaborate as in the Rome's "Gesu," Sestini eliminated the free standing,
cathedral-like pillars and columns that sectioned off the open floor plans
and presented visual obstructions to viewers. The narthex, the nave and
the sanctuary are one large, open room. The interior décor, the paintings,
the sculptures, suitable at installation, are relatively still viewed as modest
in size and not overpowering their sacred space.

After spending decades in the business of presenting and promoting fine artists, my attention always goes to the art in a church, the use of sacred images and their arrangements. Liturgical commissions now stress the importance of the congregation's attention to the main altar. Their directives follow in the lines of no distracting side altar placements, no images at the head of the church, near to the altar except those of depicting Christ incarnate, suffering, risen or triumphant.

All other images of Mary, the Mother of God, and of Saints must be placed in a sacred order in other areas of the interior where they can be devoutly recognized.

One more issue which Sestini was required to plan was the use of the images of the titular saint (Aloysius). Specifically, "many" images of the titular saint are not being presented within the same edifice except for serious reasons, and their overuse in the area of the main altar was to be avoided. Brumidi, the Artist, was commissioned by Sestini to do the masterful painting of Aloysius' First Communion for over the main altar. In addition, two other occurrences in Aloysius's story are depicted in oil tondos on either side of the praesidium arch near and widely visible to the main altar. This is not a large infraction to today's specifications, but a point of discussion about the appropriate décors of contemporary church interiors.

The 1930's renovation installation of the baptistry in the rear of the nave brought iconic Italian mosaic work and an oil wall triptych. This fine, semi-precious stone and mineral inlay will be identified later in the text. The entire, decorative wrought iron fenced enclosure was a major addition to the décor of the church; it was in keeping with the liturgical directives to make a specially designated area commensurate but not overwhelmingly distracting to its purpose. Today's architects would probably use this area of the interior for more contemporary artistic renditions of the font and its accompanying art décor to its prominent role in the liturgies.

Each of the fourteen historic, Vatican-sourced oils of the Way of the Cross on the side walls of the nave measure up to over five feet when standing on the floor. As sizable as they are they do not detract from the décor of the sanctuary and main altar, so they also fit into the parameters of modern liturgical directives. So again, the foresighted Sestini conformed to modern liturgical standards.

The Baptistry

Baptistry Within Iron Gate

The overhead reaching symmetry of the ten foot square vaults of the ceiling grab the immediate attention of the eye when entering. The grandness of the effect makes the entire interior seems larger, more cathedral-like than it actually is. Sestini's use of a repeating design and motif for the ceiling remains an appealing choice for its overall classical affect and for the aesthetic and finishing effect it adds to the whole artistic experience.

Keeping the interior clean and clear of obstructive elements is now the liturgical as well as architectural trend. Sestini was ahead of his time in this respect for he kept the interior free of standing columns and separating side aisle walls. What one sees immediately when entering is almost the volume of space of the entire interior structure except for the relatively non-intrusive, welcoming praesidium arch and the proportionately small yet visibly open side altars. The accessibility and seating in Saint Aloysius Church are reconfigured for the congregation's focus on the main altar. The present-day lighting, greatly improved to meet today's high standards, is judged by many to be glaring, too industrial or gym-like in effect and could use a lighting designer's recommendation. Natural sound carries well because of interior's open volume of space. Unfortunately, the various sound systems installed to date have been ineffective for many of the events.

A certain Mr. Frei who participated in the 1965 Liturgical Conference in Ohio made the following points in evaluating church art and architecture. "A problem in discussing art is the very difference between the written word, the spoken word, and the building or art object. In writing or speaking about visual forms, when we say, this is right, or this is wrong, we feel we are on safe ground. It is usually something we can measure and prove by objective standards. When we remark this is good or this is bad, we are apt to be discussing art. Art in the service of God and his Church have many debatable rules, important to discern. However, the mere following of all the rules does not lead to greatness.

And, I add, does not necessarily make the connection of man to God. Always the hearts and hands of a Sestini and a Brumidi and of all church architects and artists know why they do their work and for what purpose. Books like mine are only a prop or indicator to the diligence played by the creative professionals of art and architecture."

Since the earliest human beings searched for a sacred place to make a connection to the God of their understanding, they found an isolated quiet brook, a mountain top or a hillside but then began to build their own sacred spaces. Subsequently there has always been that spiritual "coupling" or blessing of earthly materials to create that separate place of solitude. "That Divine Spark" is born of the "Imagination."

The Enduring Lily: Nine Hundred North Capitol Street

It is an oddity to find an engrossing church story that contains a hook. This one does.

The hook is the Lily, the flower, used to refocus fading attention to the art and architecture in the thoughtful building of Saint Aloysius Church in 1859. The Lily, as an artist would use it in its various artistic forms, appears often in the elements of architecture and in many of the interior decorative, master paintings by the Jesuit Architect, Benedict Sestini, S.J. and Constantino Brumidi, the Master Artist, known also as the Michelangelo of the U.S. Capitol. Saint Al's still stands less than a mile from the center of the seat of this Nation.

In the serious attempt to further unveil the beauty and meaning in the art and architecture of this church, I found a visual common denominator, the Lily. It was actually used by the Artists to bind together the meaning of this historical landmark with the growth of the Federal City of Washington and at the same time used it as a poetic symbol to convey the story of the church's merited Patron, Aloysius Gonzaga, the young Jesuit who died as a youth administering to the plague victims of the 16th century.

The Lily, in this book is integral in its design; it is recognizable as it grew in symbolism in every area of the interior of the church. The Lily, symbolizing the church structure itself along with the character virtues of its Patron became a deliberate artistic element used by both the Master Architect and the Master Artist, to carry the message of their work forward to today.

Saint Aloysius Church---the Lily---has endured the events and wear of time to be a prominent inclusion in the surging and bustling far northwest edge of Washington, a once muddy, impoverished maze of alleys known as "Swampoodle," a.k.a. "puddle, puddle" in Dutch, that extended for a number of blocks in all directions.

Detail, Two Trinities painting

Lilies in the Frieze

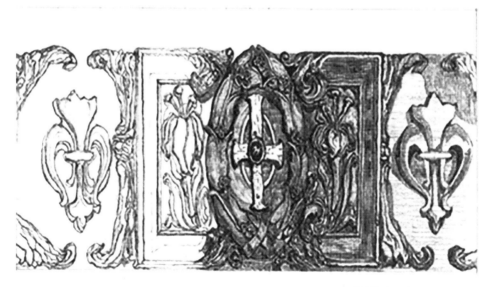

Kankanian's "Conception of Christ as the Plumb Line of Creation"

Aloysius Central Painting Removed

When this painting (approximately 11' x 15') was removed for restoration in 1993, it was carried on a flatbed truck to Page Conservation on 5th Street N.W., in Washington, D.C. That was the first time since 1859 that it was removed from its position over the main altar in the sanctuary. The original canvas was stretched tightly over a carefully constructed wood stretcher that was preserved and replaced when the restored painting was returned in 1994. The cleaned, improved and in-painted canvas is strengthened now by the application of an aluminum-type material affixed to the back of the painting. The painting was lifted into its place of honor in June of 1994, highlighted by new spotlights. The jewel in the sanctuary's crown had returned. The Gonzaga Mothers Club had raised the $40,000+ to do this preservation work.

Brumidi's Painting, Matan and Murray

Some of the colors and problems with the composition of the painting were treated as best they could be. Delicate changes added to recreate the original details of parts of the imagery. The decorative headpiece on Mrs. Douglas (her image chosen by Brumidi to represent the mother of Aloysius) was determined through close examination to be different from the original. The restoration painters brought back the original design. It is unknown why some other painter through the years had made the change from the original.

Another correction dealt with the lower right-hand area of the painting where the kneeling priest's shoes were obscured by a former restoration painter or by the pigment darkening or fading through time. It was felt that the kneeling priest was Father Villager or Father Stonestreet both well known to Brumidi and Sestini at that time. Now, the way the lower section of the canvas appears is still rather dark and the images are obscure. In considering this part of the repair, it would seem fair to judge that this part of the painting could have had better improvement. The image is just too

Renovation Watercolor Sketch by Murray

dark to be able to determine what it is. In essence, it is really the bottom soles of the two shoes of the priest, but it appears to be a large black area from a distance. We have to be aware that the original main altar design could have better accommodated the totality of the composition. Brumidi would have chosen the pigment tones in the entire painting to suit the lighting in the sanctuary. Gaslight and candlelight would have had a more subdued effect, for better or worse, on the appearance of the painting.

Pelican's Nest
Main Altar Stone and Mosaic Faceplate

That perfect, one drop of Blood falls
From the marbled-white-mosaic-feathers.

The Pelican's young open their longing bills
To be saved by the self-shed-sustenance
Into the intricately laid onyx next of aged emeralds and crimson semi-gems.

The stuff of life raises the brood
From its growing oddness
To full souls ready to take courage's wing
Into the fragile flight of life.

Guarded on all sides of its universe
Are the Four Evangelists
(Mark), The Lion, (Luke) The Eagle, (John) The Cherub, (Matthew) The Ox
Each contracted by the Word of God
To spread the exuberance
Of the Energy and revealing light
Of a better sky
To soar forever………………………..outward.

But, hardly visible because of the overwhelming interior appeal,
The Pelican, flanked by the Gospel Writers,
Is the sole reason for the art and architecture of this entire structure.
Together they form the foundation of Christianity.
They glitter and reflect with joy
To all like me
When "Introibo ad Altari Dei."

Come closer when you can
And contemplate…………………….The Pelican.

Main Altar Mosaic Façade. Pelican and Symbols of Evangelists

Brumidi's Odyssey of Art

There was everything in his works,
portraits of famous mythological figures, historical persons,
frescos of people, flowers and animals,
events renowned in Heaven and on Earth, on the Continent
and in the Americas.
Sometimes accompanied but more often alone,
Constantino conducted his painterly notes with the driving passion
of a lone eagle creating his nest.
He rushed to his passion for art.
It was a part of God's fire in his heart
that,
considered prudently,
became a Brumidi gift of art to America.
In the American culture that was hanging loose at the time,
his talents overrode criticism and boredom with the ordinary;
his previous abundant years of portable portraits and
monumental painting abroad
changed and transformed the roots of the Capitol
to rooms of poetry, spirit and historical romance.

(See Appendix, List of Brumidi's works)

Symbols of Evangelists on Main Altar Façade

Portrait of Brumidi by Nathan Leibowitz

Two Side Altar Paintings on both Sides of Praesidium Arch

"The Madonna or Mother of Sorrows," once considered an unfinished painting by Brumidi, is not signed. It was cleaned, and its frame was refurbished. It hung in the rear of the Church for many years and was moved to a more prominent place over the right-side altar in 1994. Some say it is one of Brumidi's most beautiful portrayals of Mary. It is known that the original, larger version in 1859 was an oil painting of the Madonna, much fuller in composition that was removed later for the construction to recess the side altars in the '30's. I conjecture that the same painting we now see could have been cut down from the larger canvas since the representation of Mary very closely resembles her image in the larger, original work.

The large, wood framed painting, "Holy Family in Exile in Egypt," originally had been the gift of Brumidi to Woodstock Theological College in 1868. The anonymous note we found on the canvas stretcher indicates its movement to Saint Aloysius in the 1970's. For many decades it hung in the sacristy of Saint Aloysius but was brought forward to the left side altar in 1994. Although it was not in its best condition then or now, its restoration postponed because of lack of funds at the time of the '94 Renovation. It was cleaned and some minor 'in-painting' done by the artist/architect, Armen Kankanian. There is a level of curiosity about this painting concerning its originality of composition. As is the case of the larger, center altarpiece painting, it is known that Brumidi copied great master's paintings for adoption into church venues. It appears in print to be exactly alike in color and composition to the painting we hold in Saint Aloysius.

We have always looked at the three main figures, Mary, Jesus, standing on a box or stone, and Joseph posed in a background of the pyramids with an Egyptian-like wall relief and water fountain to the left on the canvas. However, the other interpretation suggests the vertical composition of God the Father (upper part of canvas), the Holy Spirit (Dove), a little above the center of the canvas, and Jesus, (Son of God), a bit elevated from the earth by the box or stone he is standing upon. Whether viewed horizontally or vertically, the artist's intention of the Christ as the central figure is apparent. It would really be of interest to pinpoint where the Holy Family actually resided in Egypt in the length of their time of diversion. For anyone's curiosity the cost of restoring this painting now by a Master Artist to its full complement would range into five figures. Its actual monetary worth would be significant by virtue of the Brumidi's notoriety.

"The Two Trinities" by Murillo

...more on "The Two Trinities," a.k.a.," Holy Family in Egypt"

Periodically or upon occasion of an appropriate request, museums allow master painters to copy the works of great painters. Master painters are exquisitely educated to meticulously copy notable paintings. Many have done this so well that the copy is not distinguishable from the original except by experts. Often, the master copy, due to the differences in age or pigment, appears to be an improvement of the original. There are legitimate reasons in the world of art to employ master painters one of which would be to have the work seen in other areas of the world where the transportation or movement of the original is impossible.

Joseph, Detail in "The Two Trinities" by Brumidi

Brumidi, as a Master Artist, did composition copies of other known artists. Whether he obtained anyone's permission or actually was commissioned to do copies is unknown. Here, in Saint Aloysius Church, we hold the painting we have always called, "Holy Family in Egypt," done by Brumidi for the Jesuit Woodstock Theological College, Maryland and hung there in 1868. By virtue of concerned individuals, this painting found its way to St. Al's some years after the closing of Woodstock College. Recently, I discovered that it is a copy of Bartolome Esteban Murillo's, (1675-1682) "The Two Trinities," that hangs in the National Gallery, London, England.

Perhaps the least significant parts of the entire composition are in the background, the pyramids and the Egyptian head-motif water fountain. The real point of the work is the portrayal of the divine and human nature of Jesus, the central figure. Originally, Murillo did this by vertically positioning the Divine (God the Father, Holy Spirit and Son) with the horizontal representations of the Holy Family, the Human (Mary, Jesus and Joseph). This arrangement places Jesus in the central position of being Divine as well as Human whether you look down to up or side to side. He is both God and Man. Brumidi uses the pyramids and an Egyptian motif water fountain to complete his composition.

Brumidi varies the coloration a bit and gives a slightly different slant to the portraits of Mary and Joseph but just about every other aspect of the painting is the same as Murillo's version. Being a copy does not detract at all from its meaning nor aesthetic value. Its actual value is what anyone

Detail of Brumidi's God, the Father

would pay for it if offered at auction or acquisition. At that future time, a professional art agent would be employed to locate and negotiate with a real collector of this genre of painting.

Bell and Clock Tower, c.1866

Commuters and city dwellers alike, needing the time of day, always recognized the Church Tower hovering above Gonzaga. The clock presents a sweeping vista of the Swampoodle neighborhood, but the bells have lost their usage in recent decades. According to the Georgetown University Archives, a certain parish resident, Mr. B.B. French, composed the following final verses of a longer poem on Sunday morning, March 17, 1867:

Watercolor Sketch #9 by Murray

I hear those bells at morning prime
I hear them 'neath the noontides's
blazing,
But most I love the evening chime,
When they the vesper hymn are raising,
When all should bend their knee to Jesus
While tolling those Bells of Aloysius.
Ring on sweet bells, ring on and on,
Till comes that time foretold, millennial;
Till sin and woe and pain are gone,
And Man exults in joys perennial.
They shall Thy kingdom come, Lord Jesus,
And joy-bells chime from Aloysius.

The Star newspaper of September 10, 1866, reported the following description of the blessing of the bells on September 9, 1866 when the four bells, varying weight from 600 to 3600 pounds, were blessed in elaborate ceremonies:

Egyptian Decor of Fountain in "Two Trinities" Painting

Picture, if you will, the area surrounding Gonzaga College: wide, dusty F Street, lined with small stores, the church and schools. There were thousands of men, women and children to form one of the largest and most impressive religious processions ever witnessed in the City. Led by the United States Marine Band, the units began their march at three o'clock. First came the forty young men who comprised the B.F. Wiget Literary Society. Immediately following were the 600 boys and girls enrolled in the two schools of St. Aloysius Parish with their teachers. Other school children of the city joined them: 200 from nearby Immaculate Conception Schools, 40 boys from St. Joseph's Orphan Asylum, 50 girls from St. Vincent's Asylum, over 300 pupils from St. Peter's, the same number from St. Matthew's, about 250 from St. Dominic's, 400 boys and girls from Holy Trinity in Georgetown, a large delegation from St. Patrick's. Pupils from St. Mary's School went directly to the Church.

In addition, many adult groups marched also: St. Josephs Benevolent Society, St. Aloysius' Society, Young Catholic Friends Societies of both Washington and Georgetown, Catholic Total Abstinence Society and the Sodality of Immaculate Conception Church. Two other musical organizations, the Spanier Band and the Twelfth U.S. Infantry were in the line of marching. Mr. T.H. Parsons served as the Grand Marshal and received able assistance from aides scattered through the procession. They walked a route through the heart of downtown Washington – south on Ninth Street, then along Pennsylvania, Louisiana, Indiana and New Jersey Avenues, to Eye Street to St. Aloysius Church.

Archbishop Spalding from Baltimore reviewed the procession as it passed the Band Depot on New Jersey Avenue. Many distinguished citizens, including Mayor Richard Wallach, W.W. Corcoran, Orphan's Judge William F. Purcell and Joshua Register, whose Baltimore foundry cast the bells, witnessed the events from a specially-built platform in the church yard.

Each bell was inscribed to signify their donors and the person or group to whose patronage they were entrusted:

The Sacred Heart Bell weighed 3600 pounds. It read, "Alexander Provost in the year 1866 donates and dedicates this bell to the Most Sacred Heart of Jesus, Our Savior. May success and glory attend St. Aloysius Church in Washington."

The St. Aloysius Bell weighed 1800 pounds. It read, "I, George Savage, your humble servant, have erected this bell consecrated to thee, Aloysius, my heavenly patron. It announces the sacred ceremonies to be held in the church, A.D.1866."

The Blessed Virgin Bell weighed 1200 pounds. It reads, "This bell was cast as a gift from James S. Harvey, for the honor of the August and Immaculate Mary, A.D. 1866. I summon the congregation to the Church of St. Aloysius, Washington, D.C."

Church Alleyway

The Holy Angels Bell weighed 500 pounds. It read, "The boys and girls who attend the Church of St. Aloysius in Washington piously dedicate this gift of this bell to the Guardian Angels, A.D. 1866. I invoke the Angels."

Until this dedication day in 1866 the top of the tower remained empty.

It was about this same time that Brother Blasé Welch, S.J., completed installation of the now famous clock that struck every fifteen minutes. This clock was one of several Brother Welch built for a variety of Jesuit institutions. However, the Georgetown Archives shows there is no actual duplicate of the St. Aloysius clock.

A parishioner, A.N. Paresche, described it as:

A clock that will have a fourteen-foot pendulum with agate pallets. The pendulum will hang on a wall of the steeple and will be a compensation pendulum made of zinc and iron. The great features of the clock will be the movement of the pendulum

Clock Tower

and of the hands. The first will be kept in motion by a remontoir spring, connected with the escape wheel. This arrangement, as you will perceive, will render the pendulum altogether independent in its action from the going train and weight; so that whatever variations may take place in the weight, increase or decrease of friction in the train wheels, the action of the wind on the hands, want of oil, etc. will not affect the pendulum in the least. Some years ago, the clock was updated with an electrified movement.

Architectural Details by James Sanders

"Waterexpression" by Murray

Work W/C Sketch 2 by rfm

Watercolor Sketch #2 by Murray

4

Grown and Maintained in Stability

An Historical Place of the Soul

It is a building, a place, a landmark
In the Inner City in a large Nation.
It is a place of the Spirit.

This sacred place sprang to life
When it was sown in the mind and by the pen of the Architect,
Benedict Sestini, S.J., an immigrant from Italy,
A priest, Jesuit by brand, who called back into an eighteenth century
existence
An architectural style, so named "Jesuit Style,"
That is actually not a style but a quality of a place
As it carries in its bricks and stones and mortar,
An intuitive life and suggestion,
Sprouting an inner source of charisma
In a wild but fertile ground
Dedicated to become a living legend
On the same Fall October Day
President Washington's Mount Vernon
Was designated another American Landmark.

The same October Day
John Brown protested slavery
At nearby Harper's Ferry.
The seed of War
Planted a thorn in the Young Republic's side.

But the new Saint Aloysius Church
Was planted and animated by the breath of a Spirit
That germinated the inner source of strength and inspiration,

Supportive enough to make survival
To resist the fires ignited by the Blue and Grey
Blowing over
But not without fulfilling a need for a rising.

The Lily Thrives On

It was a wow moment. I knew we had completed something good. We had renewed the interior, upper church of Saint Aloysius Gonzaga on North Capitol Street in Washington. Ceremonies marking the reopening caused a fresh new wind to blow over Eye Street when the music began. There was such an element of surprise on everyone's face when the full lights came up to create the spirit that had worn away over the years to the elements, neglect and disabling situations. The spirit and soul of this great church had faded enough to doubt that such a lily could ever bloom so well again in an environment that had lost its hold on its origination, its conception and building in the middle of the 19th century. This sacred space was brought back to life again by the specific intentions and attention by close associates of the Jesuits working and carrying on their ministries in the center of the City, this Nation and the World. It is no exaggeration that joyous overwhelming feelings of awe came upon those of us who had spent nights and days the preceding years of tearing down, refashioning, painting, polishing and fixing as much as we could of what had jeopardized the future use of the place for any liturgy or event. The face of the Church of Saint Aloysius Gonzaga had been renewed and readied for use again.

Saint Aloysius Church, Design, Function and Use
Does the design of this Church and the art within fit its use?
Does its design serve as a sample of architectural art?

These two questions must be answered in this critique. Both questions get the answer of "yes" and receive the qualifier that the design, function and use partially fit the ideas for which the building was erected at the time it was built until the early 20th century. It took years for this modest, stark-appearing structure to fit the demographics of its quadrant of the City. In its earlier years, its large, sturdy, uncomplicated and unobstructed view and placement seemed out of place. However, because of its prominent visibility, it grabbed the attention of the then architects of public buildings in the City helping significantly in setting the style of architecture used for many years to come by succeeding city architects.

The liturgies conducted from the earlier years until the 1960's seemed to function well in this structure. Its traditional layout accommodated up to 1500 people at a time. The altar and sanctuary arrangement suited the variety of liturgies and events. It is easy to tell from older photos (earliest one from 1867-8) we hold that there was definite attention given to redesign and seasonal redecoration, sometime bizarre treatment of the altar. These temporary improvements of decor echo the intention to change the appearance to meet the times. No real significant change was made to the interior until the 1930's when much marble was introduced to the sanctuary areas. This improvement slightly modified the overall design.One major improvement and change to the interior floor plan came with the 1994 Renovation. The sanctuary floor was extended about 26 feet out into the nave to answer the call of more modern liturgies and bring them closer to the people. (See Liebowitz's drawing of the present floor plan). This was completed by the use of the same yellow Sienna and Travertine floor marble used in the original design. A "rolling" marble altar was newly designed, reusing two marble pedestals with inset mosaic lily decor from the former Carrera marble railing. This

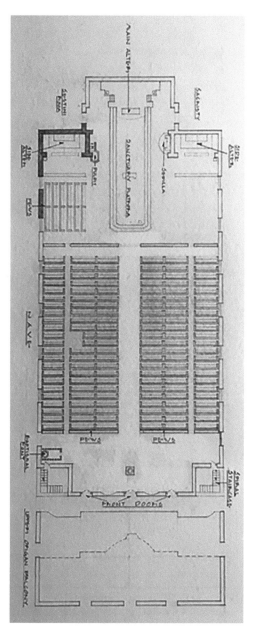

1994 Renovation Floor Plan
by N. Leibowitz

resulted in a 2,000-pound total-marble-ensemble piece (donated by R. Bratti and Son, Alexandria, Va.) that had to be lightened after its primary debut because of too much weight for the supporting floor beneath it.

The art of Brumidi has remained the same since 1859 although attention has been given to the main altar painting, sometime for the betterment with some slight detriment to the composition integrity of the original work. It was not until the 1994 renovation that Page Conservators were able to apply the latest technology to determine the original images of the painting. The Mothers Club of Gonzaga contributed $40,000+ for the work done by Page on the main altar painting and the two-side wall tondos, i.e. round oils that Brumidi originally planned to be reliefs. This work was begun by transport to Page's conservatory in Washington, D.C. and is there so documented. Recently, some 20+ years after the restoration, the Office of the Architect of the Capitol contributed their services by removing some bubbling on portions of the canvas.

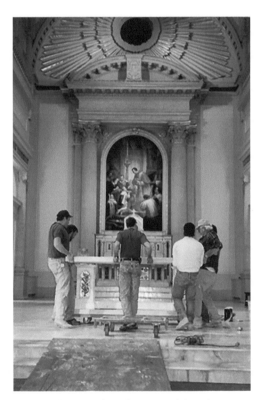

Installation of Rolling Marble Altar

Although Brumidi's works and Gagliardi's Stations of the Cross are fine works of art, their use and purposes in providing historical as well as devotional understanding for their incorporation into the interior remains a matter of opinion. It is doubtful that a modern church interior designer would choose this genre of artwork or would position it where is appears so far out of appreciative visual understanding to the viewer. It has been one of the purposes of this book to bring the characters in these paintings down and closer to the viewer by way of the fine, artistic photography of James Mathias Sanders. The more detailed and intricate and extraordinary original illustrations by Nathan Leibowitz exemplify how selected examples of the interior artwork could be rendered into single pieces of fine art in themselves.

In talking to several contemporary church architects, I discovered their inclinations to make the altar more central, less cumbersome to the space and create more fitting and dynamic stained or otherwise art glass windows to carry an aesthetic spiritual-themed message. Always, the most impressive feature of the interior is the colorful, coffered ceiling design. A contemporary idea was to do something more creative with lighting, leaving the traditional inset panels alone. All agreed that more seating was possible with different arrangements adaptable to different occasions when the church is used for concerts, lectures or other appropriate functions.

All agreed additionally that the main, large Brumidi painting would be more noticeable if brought forward into a more spectacular overhead setting with better lighting. Everyone is attracted to the openness of the interior. As it is now, the exterior architecture appears appropriate in its setting. The Clock Tower rises over the whole Gonzaga complex and for decades serves as a visual locator in Swampoodle.

The future for the church as it now stands is unknown. Presently, it is designated as the "chapel" for sole use by Gonzaga; it has ceased being a parish and may be used for weddings and funerals upon request. It is expected that the size of any newly developing parish potential will grow hugely in the next decade owing to major plans and construction of upscale residences around the Union Station, New York and Florida Avenues area and in the immediate neighborhood vicinity of the Gonzaga, Saint Aloysius complex. As a location, this part of the City of Washington has always been a changing demographic quilt requiring various uses by rotating classes of people and businesses.

Note: Statue of St. Aloysius, now in vestibule, appears on top of Baldacchino

Past Views of Sanctuary Décor

Symbol of Gospel Evangelist on Main Altar,
Photo by J. Sanders and Illustration by N. Leibowitz

It is doubtful that Ambrose Lynch, the donator of this property in the mid-1800's could have predicted what its future and that of the Jesuits themselves would hold.

"Wake up..."

"Wake up to this marvelous place" exhorted the main eloquent homilist, Walter Burkhardt S.J., "...wake up to the fresh new colors, the newly restored art work, the beauty of the architecture." Those were opening words on an early June day in 1994 when the Church of Saint Aloysius Gonzaga reopened for use after years of planning and renovation for an historical landmark that had fallen into disrepair after it had stood since its dedication in 1859. With several years' worth of steady use, the church had stood up against the weather and the elements of nature and had reached the point where definite measures were devised to save this architectural work of art designed by the Italian immigrant Jesuit priest, Benedict Sestini S.J.

As a concerned member of the working and planning committee for the renovation, I was very aware that despite my close association with the church and the school and the Jesuits had sidelined the back history of this place and the significance and stories of the art within it. It became obvious to me that we were about to put our hands on a work of art by its creators that demanded knowledge of how and why they had designed the building itself and what their reasons were for selecting the art that we see today. At the beginning of the 1991 planning time, it was expedient to move on with the actual physical renovation plans because the problems with the deterioration in the ceiling, the roof, the walls and other areas were forcing the space to close for public use. Time was the issue, and we had to save the place. Seepage of water and mold was growing more extensively. We did not have all information at hand about the original building of the structure, but we had enough to apply to the City for permissions to do some renovation and begin a fund-raising effort. By the spring of 1993, we had enough information together to request proposals from contractors and from restorers of fine paintings of historical nature.

The Renovation Committee opened its eyes to the realities of what was to be done. Better to say of what "could be done" because there was going to be a limitation on performing a complete historical restoration. I was overseeing the artistic efforts and had responsibilities to commission the five

Front and Rear View of Nave

Brumidi paintings to a proper conservator. I had to begin to determine the obvious and subtle deterioration in the paintings; in particular, the main painting over the main altar as well as the two tondos (round oils) affixed to the walls over the two side altars. The remaining two Brumidis were less important to us at that time but were not be dismissed as lesser works of art.

Kankanian at work on mural

Overall, the then present realities of time constraints and limited funds determined the scope of the work to be completed. It all pressed us to move ahead with the beginning of the tear down operations in the fall of 1993, and we finished our task by June of 1994. It seemed like a miracle to even to attempt to do this work and to have had such success in such a short time period.

Murals by Armen Kankanian in the Narthex/Vestibule

There are two wall murals painted into the niches of the vestibule. One portrays the Sacred Heart of Jesus and the other the Mother of God. Both were painted in acrylics by Armen Kankanian, Artist and Architect, commissioned to create these murals as well as to clean Brumidi's oils, "Madonna of Sorrows" and the" Holy Family in Egypt," also known as "The Two Trinities."

Armen came to America from Yerevan, Armenia in the '80's to work as an architect on a large commercial and residential project in Northern Virginia. In deciding to remain here and seek citizenship, Armen continued his career in fine painting as well as in intricate and decorative ceramic tile

Murals by Armen Kankanian; Left, "Mother of God"; Right, "Sacred Heart"

works in custom-built residences and specialized commercial projects. He is renowned today for his extensive mural work in exclusive homes and commercial enterprises.

When commissioned to do the murals in Saint Aloysius Church, he was given some indications of what the Renovation Committee hoped to see. The watercolor/pastel illustrations shown here represent the earlier concepts of what Armen proposed to do. It was one idea to move the two standing angels from the main altar area to the rear of the church, but that plan was only an interim idea. What eventually emerged are the two fresco paintings in place now.

The left-hand side mural shows a very young depiction of the Mother of God holding Jesus with an impressionist background indicating the relationship of Saint Aloysius Church to the City of Washington. There appears Gonzaga, the Capitol, and a suggestion of monuments found in the various parks. Hovering near the top and sides of the composition are the "putti" or infant angels fully focused on the central figures.

The right-hand side mural is a depiction of the Sacred Heart of Jesus holding the world globe in his hands. The background shows suggestions of the relationship of Saint Aloysius Church to the World. There is the Vatican in Rome as well as a glimpse of the Church in Yerevan personally designed by Armen. Again, the angels hover in their sole role of paying full attention on the central figure.

Both murals carry the strength and power of youth and an ease of a comfortable but commanding presence in the Narthex. Around the arch of the insets of the wall surface, Armen chose to include soft-toned depictions of architecture and his own painterly version of vaulted ceilings. The coloration is of a very definite pastel fresco and in keeping with the total idea of waking up the recessed spaces.

To finish off the ground space, the bronze gates from the marble communion rail that were moved to make space for the extended platform of the Sanctuary, were centrally positioned on the new marble floor and flanked by marble sections or columns from the communion rail.

It was noted that the paint on the murals has steadily encountered a peeling and flaking problem caused by dampness that creeps in – an ongoing situation with a building of this vintage. The results frequently require additional in-painting to portions of the image.

Perhaps in time, a fuller appreciation for these Italian masterpieces will be more evident if repositioned in an appropriate lighting venue.

Armen Kankanian, Muralist and Fine Artist

Kankanian Mural. "City of Washington, St. Aloysius in background"

The Vatican, Detail from Vestibule Mural

Stations of the Cross Paintings from Rome

The details, value and story of these paintings have gone unnoticed for a long time. They deserve to be rediscovered.

The progressive series of fourteen paintings depicting Christ's movement on the Via Dolorosa by Italian artist, Gagliardi, were presented by the Vatican in Rome as a gift to Saint Aloysius Church in 1878. It is reported that the artist, knowing one day that the Pope was going to be meeting a crowd in the Vatican Square, personally carried the Twelfth Station (Crucifixion) to a location where the Pope blessed it. This story is presented in full a little later on in this text.

These oils are realistic versions of that dark saga. Like many works of the subject matter, they are not as grotesque as the event they represent, but are traditional paintings telling the story. Unfortunately, on the walls of Saint Aloysius Church they fall out of their vibrancy that we clearly saw when they were relocated for cleaning. The dim light from the stained-glass windows does not do justice to these works nor do the present lighting fixtures underneath them. Originally, in 1859, they were gas lighted in fan-like- looking fixtures giving a subtle light to each painting. The new but inadequate fixtures, added in the '94 Renovation were a failure in highlighting what we had hoped to perform. Admittedly, the dark backgrounds in each composition keep the finer details in these paintings very subdued to the eye.

Stations of Cross

Stations of Cross

Selected Scenes from Way of The Cross Paintings
By Gagliardi (Rome)

Paintings like these resemble much 19th century church art. They are decorative, relatively calm in composition with intentional degrees of restrained sensitivity given to the subjects and the situations they portray. For instance, there is a particular sensitivity paid to the action between Christ and the women of Jerusalem. The horror of these followers of Jesus experience and became real by the fine brushwork of the Artist as he sets up the action of the scene. Each station painting is a meditation in itself, and it must have been for the artist as he proceeded down his own path to the completion of the fourteenth finale in rendering the only grave site ever to be emptied on this earth   We are probably witnessing repeatedly the artist's own passion prayer in his work. Perhaps in time, a fuller appreciation for these Italian masterpieces will be more evident if repositioned in an appropriate lighting venue.

The following is *An Incident in the History of the Stations of the Cross at St. Aloysius* found in the Georgetown University Archives, pp. 416-19. No one is identified by name other than Pope Pius IX and the article's author is anonymous also.

An important art addition to the interior of the Upper Church was made in the mid-point of the 1870's. A modern Italian Painter, Gagliardi, was commissioned to execute the Stations of the Cross for St. Aloysius' Church. By the end of Spring of 1875 he had finished seven of the paintings and shipped them to Washington. The remaining canvases were in various stages of completion when a group of touring Washingtonians visited Gagliardi's Roman studio. As they examined the paintings a sudden, happy thought struck. The patron feast of the church in which these works would hang was only a short time away. Would it not be a unique privilege for them to carry the blessing of His Holiness, Pope Pius IX? Quickly the artist agreed with the Americans, promising to complete at least one more canvas by June 21. He kept his word, and on the eve of the appointed day delivered the twelfth station, The Crucifixion, to the tourists' hotel. Italians, when learning of such an audacious plan, were shocked, but this did not deter the visitors.

Early on the morning of June 21 they set out for the Vatican, bearing "a floral decoration about three feet high, composed entirely of yellow and white flowers, the papal colors, hidden among which was an offering for the Holy Father." A servant carrying the gaudily gilt-framed twelfth station brought up the rear of the procession. The unidentified Americans had no tickets of audience for this day, one of great importance since it represented a double celebration: The Feast of St. Aloysius Gonzaga and the anniversary of the coronation of Pius IX. Hence, they did not expect to be present when the Holy Father bestowed his blessing. They planned instead simply to contact Monsignor Bede Mervoe, a member of the Vatican staff and personal friend, and ask him to take the painting to His Holiness. While waiting in an anteroom at the Vatican, however, their plans were abruptly changed. A Roman nobleman of their acquaintance (also unidentified) happened on the scene and insisted that the Americans themselves present the art work to the Pope. Escorting them to a large room along one of the main corridors in the Vatican Palace, their Italian friend explained that the Holy Father would come along this hall enroute from an audience and they could then make their request in person. The foreigners felt a bit nervous, needless to say, but soon forgot their own shakiness when they heard a slight rustle in the corridor. Pope Pius IX, with colorfully attired entourage, suddenly came into the room, greeted American children, accepted their offerings and blessed the picture for the Church of St. Aloysius belonging to the Jesuit Fathers of Washington. The members of his court expressed their pleasure at the gifts in another way, for they "began to strip the floral offering to adorn their buttonholes with yellow and white flowers."

On the Streets of Jerusalem

In the middle of the clamor of such a mission-climb to Golgotha
Into the deadly net of human error,
Yet victoriously completing His passion resurrection,
Through divine reality and kindness,
on to the stone streets,
stumbles the Messiah.

The sad beast of the Holy Burden
passionately paws on his stony stand,
pulling at his tether
while the muffled shouts of the crowd
cry out for the burden
the mule may no longer be allowed to bear.

Salvation happens in city streets
where exists thought and ideas
along with solitude and loneliness,
where fellowship becomes intimacy,
where diversity meets cooperation,
where crime counters generosity,
the good with no good.
Salvation breaks through
frantic clouds of one dark- Jerusalem- city- day.

Each one in his own way
grasps the experiences brushed onto these fourteen canvases
of the lament and horror
on the faces of the city's people
viewing the rising dust from the crude cross
dragging along, digging up the dirt of salvation.
City faces—stunning faces, naturally appealing
faces, bearded, broad, narrow and stern faces;
faces of the feminine yearning with disbelief.
The rabid mob moves upward.

Fleeting glances from questioning faces, pale in
fright
of the sight of Him hitting and losing ground.

Detail Stations of Cross

The Face in the shroud
is offset in the reach of a singular spiritual act;
a Face voided of human dignity,
barely missing the hot flanks of a stallion,
pulled back by an ironclad face.

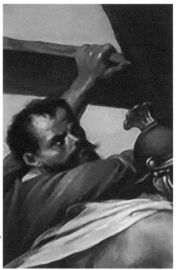

The ageless, sacred face of a Woman grimaces
at the increasing grind of pain.

And from above all these City faces and doleful masks
emerges the ground-smeared Face of a full-blown lily,
the favored prize of divine will,
advancing to its final display in the container of salvation,
Calgary.

The raw bitter splendor of the passion would become apparent in time, washing
away, but exposing Eternal Life.

Many who come here to Saint Al's
trudge their own soul's way
beneath these ageless works of art,
not fully aware of the artist's visual power
to expose the message of this structure's
commanding facade
rising firmly above the ground
in this Inner City, the Nation
and in this World.

Detail Stations of Cross

People of Jerusalem

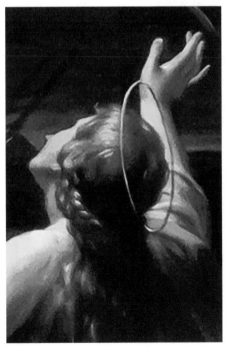

Ceiling Panel with Cross; Mary Magdalene

People of Jerusalem

Weeping women of Jerusalem

Bystander at Crucifixion

Roman Soldier

The Triduum

1993-1994 Renovation Underway

5

Standing with Dignity, Strengthened by Care

(top balcony over vestibule)

Fantasy and fugue, organ tones below powerfully into the nave, apse and
sanctuary and into every corner of the church lightly-awakened by the
radiant rays through the stained- glass in the mid- morning April sun.
The huge moment fills with the spiritual power and a depth of sternness
from the organist's artistry of the Bach Easter Oratorio.

The church turns into an abode for inner refuge of an unrealized yearning for God, for the revealing experience a service in Saint Aloysius Church can bring when utilized to its maximum.

Considering Church Architects

Overall, architects of church structures and related landscapes will create an inner form of their work, bringing the essence of their imaginations and designs to actuality. They will create a structure from their intellects. Creation implies taking a stand. Thereby the abstract or spiritual relationships of their visions are brought to evidence.

That realization of what they have created, the development of it in stones, bricks, mortar, plastics, woods, glass etc., is of a metaphysical transformation into materials of the essence of things.

'93-'94 Renovation underway

That process of creativity will penetrate into the depths of the architects, and related other artists, by their intuitive artistic senses that develop into their primary purpose for embarking in this kind of architectural endeavor... a connection with God.

Some architects, not all, create structure and places that are lasting depending on the elements of nature and the continuing care of a thinking people.

The Overall Impression

Strong but soft
cheerful colors decided
the forming fingers
of the artists and architect
making this place
happen in this City.

It was pre-Civil War time
when horses and slaves
would soon serve other masters
while a few dedicated men
continued to teach, to pray
and
to serve every honorable cause.

Washington's street mud ran red
from the blue and the gray
while St. Al's remained open in prayer
for a brighter day.

Architectural Detail over Sanctuary
by James Sanders

Brumidi

His ideal content
of the spiritual world,
infinitely rich and colorful,
always consistent
in style and multiform,
is reproducible
to a thought-painting.
Its realization succeeds
as the resources of a creative mind
of the language of the visual arts,
the instrument of his soul's expression.
It proves the painting-aware meditation
In a constructive, orderly thought pattern
In the uniting of the historical
and
the spiritual.

Brumidi's art,
fused with
Sestini's architecture,
accomplishes its lasting imprint,
landmarking North Capitol Street.

Work W/C Sketch 8 by rfm

Gold Mosaic Risers Between Sanctuary Steps

Church Architect - Sestini

In the beginning of his days
in a universe of Jesuits,
God gives him intuitive,
life giving, unique talents
to break through and surpass
many spheres of creativity.

The chaos of a young City wants to clear
as the Architect sets about unfolding the plans
in accordance with preconceived plans
to build an edifice on a street
suiting its time and all times,
a place to teach
and care
for the body and the soul.

Work W/C Sketch 10 by rfm

"Taking Shape" by N. Leibowitz

The Wall Frieze around the Nave

To the left as you enter the Narthex, there is a small, preserved portion remaining of the original decorative wall frieze that surrounds the entire nave. Brumidi hired some of his apprenticed artisans, who were working at that time on the Capitol Building, to paint in his design for the wall over the pews, of Saint Aloysius Church. This design is frequently referred to as "Abundance" and has been for many decades a popular decorative theme in public buildings and homes. In the Capitol Building itself, there is an elaborate stairway banister in iron or bronze of similar floral-leaf design.

Watercolor Sketch by Murray

The coloration of this original portion of the frieze (near the Baptismal area) suggests a tan background with muted tones of green and gold to complete the design. For some reason in the mid 1900's, probably during the 1959 Renovation effort, the frieze was covered over with a green faux marbled type of laminated material that was impossible to remove during the 1993/4 Renovation without pulling away a great deal of the original frieze design and color.

To continue our purpose of returning to the original design of the frieze, the noted church decorative painter, Bob Thuman, made an exact stencil of the original design pattern; as the stencil was applied around the nave, it was painted with new tones of tan, beige and gold and highlighted in gold leaf where the design graduated to its fullest form revealing a basket bearing fruits and flora etc. Each one in the working Renovation Committee was afforded the opportunity to apply with brush in hand his own personal touch to this new version of the original frieze.

Bob Thuman, Church Decorative Master Artist

The result of this new version of the wall frieze brought a brighter and more captivating surround to the entire nave of the church. It helped pick up the natural light in the interior as well as lift the eye upwards to the windows and towards to sanctuary and side altars that needed more brightness and visual focus.

There was some consideration given to continuing using this "Abundance" design on the wall to the right and left of the main altar in the sanctuary, but it did not happen. One reason was that we were attempting to simplify the décor in the Sanctuary to bring as much attention as possible to the newly restored main altar painting of Saint Aloysius. It is very evident in the photos from the original and several succeeding years that the Main Altar décor was much more ornate and complicated than it is today. One can see there were many more painted wall décors as well as two niches on either side of the main altar's iron pilasters. It appears that the statues in these former niches varied from era to era. As acceptable and more elaborate as the 1859 décor of the Sanctuary was regarded, the '94 Renovation Committee wanted to "contemporize" the sanctuary area to lessen distraction to the liturgies to be performed on the newly extended sanctuary floor with a backdrop and emphasis on Brumidi's painting of Aloysius and the Eucharist.

Windows of Clear and Art Glass

Once clear glass panes in 1859
Sent the northern days light to the interior nave.

Twenty years later, jewel-colored glass of geometric design threw dimensions of variations of light
onto the solid oak pews and carpeted floors.

In every era, luminous traces of an artist's image thought, a world of his own concepts, translated the sun's light into inexhaustibly rich tones,
endlessly polymorphic.

The windows have their own spirit of an imaginative created image of a skilled artist of glass could foresee.

On the street front, the window stained glass, away from the large windows in the nave.

Contractor's Proposal Drawing

A drawing in contractor's proposal
displaying a façade of windows with an opacity like the famed Meyer
glasswork
found throughout other churches and residences of the 1800's.

The thought occurs --- what window design would Sestini
prefer if there had been funds
enough to complete his wishes?
Nature's morning and the late afternoon light
effects a more meditative mood
for those who come to visit, to simply rest or to pray.

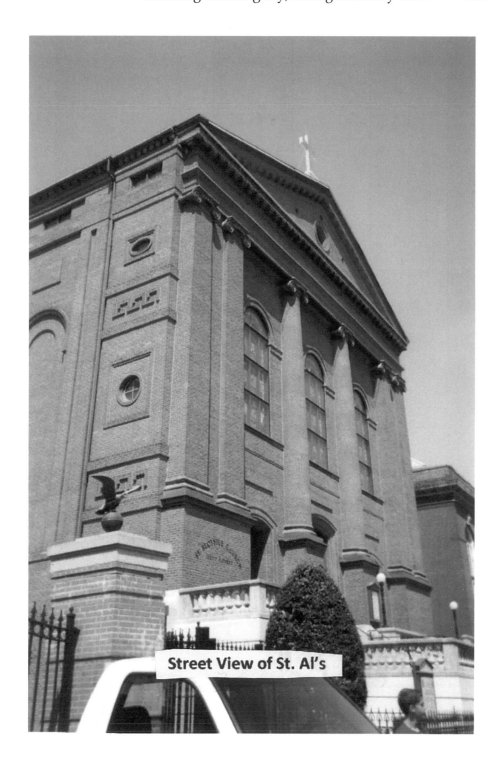

Street View of St. Al's

Balcony North Capitol Street Window

Nave Window

Detail in Altar Painting

Relief of Lilies in Ceiling Frieze

Marble Lily Detail in Aloysius Sculpture in Vestibule

Lilies in the Architecture

An apparent Architect's ploy -
An array of plaster swirling branches, leaves
and blossoms,
rambling visibly
in a flowering order
of unity and integrity.

Entwined and imbedded
with diverse shapes and forms of churchly lilies,
incantations of the Eucharist
absorb the Dignity, Integrity
and Stability of all youth.

The Ceiling

Abstracted into cubes
of ivories and blues,
a greatly timbered flying structure
reveals itself
in a new way,
strikingly true to its essence as a cover.

The solidly-jointed,
concealed redwood beams,
connecting the gilded fleur-de-lis assemblage,
bring the architect's dream of a heaven
to hover above
this sacred, soil-richly-connected
City Place.

The Way of Sorrow

In the midst of such a mission
to Calvary,
caught in the deadly net
of human error,
still victoriously completing
a resurrection
through reality and kindness, He,
the Messiah,
assumes his own task of human experience,
throughout these Vaticanesque oil depictions,
with the pathos and the sorrow, step by step
to the hill of the cross.

Many who come here
walk the walk
from one to fourteen,
few are aware of
their power
in sealing this building's purpose
solidly
to the ground
in the City, the Nation, the World.

Watercolor Working Sketch by Murray
"Madonna of Sorrows"

The Tondos

Courtly-clad figures and faces
in paintings of princely, prayerful ways
float with saintly dreams
over the pair of mounted tondos,
ordering and passing through
motions and stories
of the Blessed Aloysius.

Terry Matan Observes Tondo Restoration

The Madonna

"Madonna" Oil by C. Brumidi

In precious moments
a painting-thought,
conceived in rare brilliance
with depth,
enters the Artist's inner eye,
condenses itself,
assumes a definite form,
completes itself
fulfilling its meaning
in a master's work of art
to become
"Madonna of Sorrows."

The Sanctuary of Saint Aloysius Church*

Sanctuary Floor

There are three architectural areas of the interior of this, basically, Romanesque style building, the vestibule – where you enter, the nave – the main body of the church and the sanctuary - the altar area. The sanctuary as it is today, is the result of the 1934 and 1994 renovations to the floor, the marble altar and the intricate mosaic work. The altar painting by Constantino Brumidi, the jewel in the crown, has been there since the opening of the church in 1859. This is an elaboration of the fine stone and mosaic work in the sanctuary.

The marble flooring of the Sanctuary is composed mainly of Roman Travertine marble that is found in that portion of Italy known as Lazio where the Eternal City is situation.

Travertine marble has a traditional and historical background, as it is said that the ancient Roman ruins that are to be seen to this day, were originally built with Travertine and on them many Christians shed their blood. Therefore, it is appropriate for use in the Roman Catholic Church, especially so in the Sanctuary.

When quarried it is fairly soft and very porous but quickly hardens when exposed to the air and is considered by most architects the ideal material for flooring and wainscoting.

* From *The Jubilee Program of St. Aloysius Church, Washington. D.C., 1858-1934*,
Press of W.F. Roberts Co., Washington, D.C.
Appendix C. "The New Sanctuary," pages 101-104.

In the main part of the flooring there are three squares of a carpet tile type of another species of Travertine known as Antique Siena. The soil apparently is much richer which accounts for the dark, almost grained color of this marble with occasional bits of petrified vegetation which are found upon minute examination. This is extracted from the Siena district of Tuscany.

Bianco Porracci and Negro del Belgio fashion the marble border in a herring bone pattern. Bianco Porracci marble is first quality marble from the Carrara district in the famous Apuane Alps which are situated not far from the old cities of Pisa and Lucca. This marble is used extensively for Statuary purposes and combined with Altissimo and the Statuario marble is considered the choicest of all found in the world.

The Negro del Belgio, or as it is better known as Belgian Black, is quarried not far from the famous old town of Ypres. The quarry operations in that marble were suspended early during April 1914, at the time of the invasion, and were again resumed in 1920. Its demand increased because of the limited supply, and the few remaining blocks were carefully withheld from the market for years and later offered under the name of Black Onyx which is used extensively in the manufacture of semi-previous jewelry. The broad band which encompasses the entire floor and step risers is composed of yellow marble known as Giallo di Siena, famous throughout the world for its beauty. Important installations can be found in most of the finest churches in Italy including St. Peter's in Rome. It is practically the main scheme of decoration for the famous Cathedral of Sienna. The Cathedral and Archdiocese were presided over until 1908 by the great Cardinal Tommasi who was the paternal uncle of Giuseppe Tommasi, the artist who created and designed this particular Flooring, Pulpit, and Sedilia, and supervised their execution in the Italian Studio, precisely in Pietrasanta where this work was done.

All the risers of the steps along the Sanctuary, including those of the High Altar, are executed by a very ancient guild with its studio on the Grand Canal in Venice and are composed of thin layers of pure gold 24K, hand beaten and laid upon a slab of molten glass, then covered with another coating of glass forming a protection of the gold which will never tarnish. The most famous collection of Venetian glass mosaic will be found in the famous Basilica of St. Mark in Venice.

The last and most interesting of the composition of the flooring are the inlaid panels executed in the world famous Florentine Mosaic. These panels were made by a small Guild, practically unknown outside of Italy, located on the Piazza di Santa Croce in the very house where the Immortal Dante lived centuries ago. This Guild was founded in the days of Medicis and had the patronage of the great Princes and Cardinals of the Church, and flourished for many centuries.

Florentine mosaics are, as known, composed completely of minute pieces of natural marble, each one selected for its own particular degree of quality and of coloring, and carefully inlaid into a larger slab to form a perfect picture reproduction. The execution of even the smallest objects takes weeks and sometimes months of painstaking toil on the part of many men. In many instances gold, silver, Mother of Pearl, Lapis Lazuli, Carnelian Jasper and other semi-precious stones are used.

Twenty-three Karat Gold Leaf Mosaic, Main Step Risers

Pictured in Florentine Mosaic in the floor is the Coat of Arms of the family of Gonzaga together with five of the seven Sacrament symbols, namely Baptism Confirmation, Penance, Holy Orders and Extreme Unction. The symbols for Holy Eucharist and Matrimony were executed in Florence and donated by the Notre Dame Sisters. The Eucharist symbol was inlaid set near the Sedilia and the Matrimony symbol on the pulpit side.

Baptism

Confirmation

Eucharist

Holy Orders

Reconciliation

Sanctuary Floor Mosaic Symbols of Sacraments

The pulpit and sedilia (bench) were executed in select light Botticino marble which was extracted from the quarry situated in the vicinity of Rome. This marble with its soft, warm, buff-gray tone, harmonizes with the sanctuary flooring. The large panels in front and on the side of the pulpit, as well as on the sedilia, are inlaid with Cream Algerian Onyx. This beautiful onyx, found in Algeria, with its golden veining gives a rich appearance to all work. When sawed across the bed stratum (it gives the unusual veining which runs vertically in the Pulpit and horizontally in the Sedilia)

Red Languedoc, a French marble is used in the front lower panel of the pulpit, and Alps green, Italian marble is inlaid in a geometrical design. The herring bone pattern border in blue and gold surrounding the Algerian Onyx panels is Venetian mosaic, and the same mosaic in red and gold compose a circular border inlaid in the center panels of both the pulpit and sedilia.

The five carved bas-reliefs inlaid in the front panel of the pulpit are sculpted in Bianco Porraci and represent the four Doctors of the Church; the center panel is a carved Dove (Holy Spirit). The open book carved on the reading desk with the letters A.M.D.G. signifies the motto of the Jesuit Order – "To the Greater Glory of God."

Gonzaga Family Crest

The sedilia is made with Florentine mosaic – itself a masterpiece of the medium. A major improvement in the 1994 renovation was the extension of the sanctuary floor approximately 26 feet into the center of the nave. It is composed of the same travertine marble used in 1934 and comes from the same Italian quarry. The border of this extension is of the same yellow Sienna marble as used previously.

To embrace the new liturgy, a rolling portable altar was constructed of a marble top table supported by the original communion railing pedestals that held the gates to the sanctuary. However, it was later determined that this 2,000-pound addition was too heavy for the floor and another lighter weight marble top replaced it and lightened the load by 1,100 pounds. The altar is rolled or moved now depending on the types of liturgies or events taking place.

One amazing note should be made to the over-life-sized, many ton, Carrara marble statue of St. Aloysius that stands now in the vestibule at the entrance. There are existing photos that show this huge piece was originally placed on top of the altar's Baldachino – the back drop being the stained-glass sunburst window behind it. We do not know when it was moved to the floor, but it must have been sometime around or before the 1934 renovation. The sculpture depicts Aloysius in liturgical vestments holding a crucifix interwoven with lilies.

Note too that the original altar and communion railing was of finely carved Phillipino Mahogany – a small remnant remains.

The New Baptistry Donated by the Church Sanctuary Society in the '30s

The marble platform is composed mainly of a newly discovered Travertine marble, Rosa Villanova, imported for the first time in 1859. It is found in Tuscany, Italy, and particularly in the hills Colle Val D'Elsa (Siena). From this same section is quarried the world known Golden Yellow Siena marble used in the narrow border of the platform. It has also been used for the steps and the broad band in our Sanctuary marble flooring. The riser and the main border of the platform is the famous real Rosso Levanto which is extracted from the mountains surrounded by the Gulf of La Spezia, Italy, situated on the Tyrrhenian Sea, between Leghorn and Genoa. The mar-

Mosaic and Marble Relief of Dove on Pulpit

New Baptismal Font Donated by St. Al's Sanctuary Society in the 1930's

ble ribbon border is executed in Bianco Altissimo and Belgian Black. Bianco Altissimo is the white marble quarried from the Apuane Alps which surround the town of Petrasanta (Holy Stone) near Carrara, Italy. It receives that name of Altissimo because it is found at the highest point of the Apuane Alps. It is an historical fact that the great Michelangelo opened the road to the quarry by order of Pope Giulio II, who gave him the financial support needed. With the biggest first block of marble quarried, he executed one of his masterpieces, the statue of Moses. Recently it has been discovered, upon careful examination, that the face of Pope Giulio II is discernible in the beard. The baptismal font is made entirely of Mandorlato

Font Pedestal

St. Ambrogio, which is extracted from the mountains surrounding the city of Vicenza, situated in Northern Italy. With its rich soft rose coloring this marble is most appropriate for the purpose of the font.

On the six pilasters supporting the font beautiful Onice Piemonte (Piedmont Onyx) panels are inserted with a geometrical border of a new type of Venetian mosaic. Instead of using one color, it is sprayed over with various colors and covered with another coating of glass for preservation. The bowl portion of the font above the pilasters is enriched with six Florentine marble mosaic panels with a Venetian mosaic border the same as the pilasters. The symbols used on the panels starting from the front left pilaster are: The Fountain of Life, The Ark of Noah, The Opening Rocks and The Torrents of Water (Moses striking the Rocks), A Dove (The Holy Spirit), A Fish, A Shell. The spaces between these panels are incised, gilded and

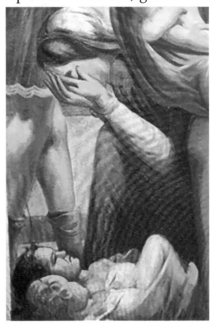

inscribed, "The Spirit, The Water, The Blood, These Three Are One: John v.8." Fine carving throughout the base and the bowl completes an unusual artistic effect.

The credence table and bench are executed in Botticino marble with inserted panels of cream Algerian Onyx with the new type Venetian mosaic geometrical border in green and gold, with another type of mosaic having a rough service. The drawer is of old oak with rich inlay of contrasting woods. The wainscoting marble dado is made of Breccia Auroa. The base is Verde Bottiglia (Bottle Green) and the top in dark Portasanta (Holy Door).

Details from Paintings Over the Font Depicting Three Forms of Baptism

Elegant Italian Mosaic Baptismal Symbols on Font

Underside of Baptistry Lid

All these marbles are quarried in Piedmont, Italy. The cover and inside bowl of the font are made of red bronze. The outside surface of the cover, when closed, conforms to a sphere with a marble bowl. It is ornamented with designs of stars, sun rays, moon beams and water, and in the center, stands out the cross, the symbol of Christianity, surmounting the world. The ornaments are carried out by craftsmen in relief style to the finest degree of perfection. The inner surface of the cover is flat and depicts, in the form of a cross, the first baptism in the River Jordan. The figures of Christ and St. John and the background are heavily hand-engraved into the surface, with the important lines accentuated by darkening. At each corner are cherubs delicately detailed and surrounding the entire motif in the form of a border are the words: "I baptize thee in the name of the Father and of the Son and of the Holy Ghost." These are deeply cut into a surrounding band. The surface is polished with a bright finish with an enameled background of cerulean blue and the lettering in crimson. When opened a beautiful effect is produced. A device is provided which keeps the cover in a vertical position when opened.

Underside of Baptismal Font Lid

The outside is finished in dark statuary bronze which lends dignity to this fine example of hand wrought bronze art. The bowl, finished in rose gold, into which the water flows, is removable. This has been hand-hammered into its shape. The receptacle for the holy water, holy oils and cotton is in the form of a shell, an artistic gem in itself.

The wrought iron grille around the baptistry is executed in Swedish coal iron which is the best of its kind for artistic wrought iron work. All the iron is hand-hammered and forged including the decorative and ornamental parts. At the lower part of the grille there are circular panels with a shield in the center. Around the panels are alternate artistic treatments of laurel and oak leaves, indicative of peace, glory and power. The small square panels contain decorative designs of the lily of innocence alternatively linked with twisted rings. Above, in the lower frieze the mystic rose is used as ornamentation. The symbols in the shield are done in relief style as follows: The three Theological Virtues consisting of a cross for Faith, an anchor for Hope, a heart and candle for Charity. On the front is the threefold nature of Christ; a censor for the Priest, a scepter for the King and the myrrh tree for the Prophet. On the right side nearest the pews are the three Evangelical Counsels, poverty represented by coins at bare feet, Chastity by a lily, and obedience by a chalice.

The columns above the lower portion are twisted and ornamented with decorative leaves. In the top frieze of the grille, sun flowers and leaves are used as ornamentation. The top portion contains a decorative cresting as a design, and in the center front there is a shield with ribbon and crown. The symbol of this is a hand and a cloud, Dextera Dei. All the wrought iron has a Swedish finish which renders it bright and rustproof.

The design of the baptistry is due to the creative genius of the architect, Giuseppe Tommasi, the same man who designed the new sanctuary marble flooring. He designed and made the full-sized details and selected the materials used for the baptistry expressly for our church. Therefore, for the originality of the design of the Baptismal Font, which is absolutely distinctive, the plans were registered in the Copyright Office of the United States in Washington. The com-

Above Entrance to Baptistry Area

Tommasi studio signature at base of angel sculpture in sanctuary

mission of the Baptistry was carried out by the Giuseppe Tommasi Studio of New York City. All of this marble work was executed in their studio in Pietrasanta, Italy, under the personal supervision of the artist, Tommaso Tommasi, brother of Giuseppe. The wrought iron and bronze work was done in New York City.

The font and baptistry were blessed and dedicated on the Feast of the Immaculate Conception, 1934. The font and furnishings are the gift of the Dore family in memory of their parents. The grille is the gift of the Sanctuary Society.

Details of Angels in Sanctuary

The Tommasi Studio engaged the celebrated artist, Ilario Panzironi, to paint in oil a beautiful mural representation of the threefold baptism (Water, Blood, Desire), to adorn the baptistery. It was the gift of Miss Katherine C. Babbington, in memory of her parents, William and Bridget Babbington. (Note here this is the same Tommasi Studio who created the two marble praying angels on either side of the main altar.)

Dedicated Bells
As the St. Al's 75th Anniversary Program Presented Them

The general work of renovation and restoration undertaken on the occasion of the Diamond Jubilee revealed a dangerous leaning condition of the belfry above the great Clock due to the wear and tear of the elements. This condition called for immediate attention, and the firm of McCloskey and Company, engaged in several major construction operations in Washington, was engaged to completely rebuild that part of the belfry above the clock. The former construction was wholly of wood; the belfry as reconstructed consists of a massive steel frame with concrete base for the bell stands and wheels. This frame is enclosed with wood, and the whole is encased in copper, and surmounted by an iron cross similarly covered. During this operation the clock was stopped, and the bells of St. Aloysius were silenced, both being very much missed by all in the vicinity of the church.

The clock, for years, guided the lives and the activities of homes and shops and offices for miles around, and the bells tolled off the hours and halves and quarters with precision surpassed by no other timepiece. It was one of the several famous clocks made by Brother Blasé Walsh, S.J., who had an art all his own which seems to have died with him when he passed to his reward in old Frederick town, June 2, 1897.

However, when even this faithful old clock began to fail from age and its master was no longer available to repair and restore it, and no other layman could do so, the Fathers were fortunate to have found in Father Joseph Johnson, S.J., a missionary in St. Mary's County since 1922, one who understood the intricacies of the clock and who quickly and quietly set it going again. When the clock and bells were out of service while the belfry was being rebuilt the following story was told of the Gonzaga clock in a news item:

Illustration by N. Leibowitz

There is in the bell tower of St. Aloysius' Church here a famous old clock, which to many in the National Capital is immensely more important that the amazingly accurate timepiece at the Naval Observatory. The clock, a huge affair, is said to have no counterpart in this country, or probably the world. It is more than sixty years old, the work of a Jesuit Brother, and has played an intimate and faithful part in the daily lives of thousands of the city's residences. Once, it is said, it was used to check the arrival and departure of trains from Washington, and was the timepiece by which all clocks in the Capital were regulated. Brother Blasius Walch, S. J., a native of Europe, made the famous 'Gonzaga clock,' as well as clocks at Woodstock, Md. Loyola College, Baltimore; Fordham University, New York; Boston College, and St. Andrew-on-Hudson, Poughkeepsie, N.Y. No two of these clocks are alike.

The bells were forged in the Joshua Register foundry in Baltimore. Archbishop Spalding consecrated them on Sunday afternoon, September 9, 1866, and Catholics from all parts of the city assembled for the ceremony. A parade led by the Marine Band formed at the old College on Ninth and F Streets. The route followed Ninth Street to Pennsylvania Avenue to Louisiana, to Indiana, to New Jersey, to Eye Street to the church grounds.

Sodalities and various Catholic Societies, numbering about 700, were in line and Sunday School children to the number of 2300, from St. Aloysius (600), Holy Trinity (400), St. Patrick's, St, Peter's St. Matthew's, St. Dominic's and St. Mary's. Father Wiget, then Pastor and Father Roccofort, Master of Ceremonies, were in charge of the arrangements in the great space to the North of the Church. Archbishop Spalding reviewed the parade as it passed the B. and O. Station, then on New Jersey Avenue. After the consecration of the bells he addressed the vast throng, dwelling on the significance of the beautiful ceremony; that at the sound of the bells, Almighty God would move the hearts of His people and attract them to His temple to hear the preaching of His truth and lift their souls to Him in praise and prayer.

Because the bells have been silent for many years, I want to re-emphasize their history and importance with the hope that they will be heard again.

The Sacred Heart bell weighs 3,600 pounds. It is too heavy to be hung by rope and wheel, but it is rolled by means of a hammer for the Angelus and

De Profundis. The Blessed Virgin's bell weighs 1,200 pounds; the St. Aloysius 1,800 pounds, and the Holy Angels' bell, 500 pounds. The Inscriptions are as follows:

"Alexander Provost (the donor) in the year 1866 donates and dedicates this bell to the Most Sacred Heart of Jesus, Our Savior. May success and glory attend St. Aloysius' Church in Washington."

"This bell was cast as a gift of James S. Harvey, for the honor of the August and immaculate Mary, A.D. 1866. 'I summon the congregation to the Church of St. Aloysius, Washington."

"I, George Savage, your humble client, have erected this bell consecrated to thee, Aloysius, my heavenly Patron. It announces the sacred ceremonies to be held in thy church, A.D. 1866."

"The boys and girls who attend the Church of St. Aloysius in Washington piously dedicate the gift of this bell to the Guardian Angels. A. D. 1866. 'I invoke the angels.'"

Aloysius Ab Angelis*

Only Known Photo of Original Sculpture Décor over Main Altar

And they regarded him as a noble's son
From the shadows of their minor thrones,
A very fine boy exceptional to see
With a special fervor for life
Composed of all that was the enviably good,
Well born, well received,
This mannered boy, Luis.

What an extraordinary embarrassment to the cultured kind
He would turn to be,
Removing himself from wealth to a life of the spirit.

*Translated – "He was not the least among the angels."

Turning with head turned forward
To a life within a burdened church
That would quickly take his life away.

From his knees to his weakened feet,
From contemplation into action,
At 23 years, though young but fevered,
Aloysius befalls with hands soiled in the service of another man's plague.

Now here his memory exists, the namesake of a church,
Among a host of lilies on canvas, brick and stone,
Intent and sporting the blue cape of a humanity,
Professes a higher purpose to a powerful world.

Aloysius, a really fine boy, you really could not have known
How and for what America would know you.
As it was once stated,
"Monumenti Eum
Paulo Minus
Ab Angelis"

From the 1867 inscription in the sculptural arrangement above the original altar.
Also, Brumidi's two tondos established Aloysius in the company of the angels.

Angel Illustration by Nathan Leibowitz

Altar, Framed in Strength

Architectural Details

Standing strong and stable,
They flank the onyx-enhanced altar table,
deeply fluted iron columns of iron
and rise
in a surround to Brumidi's portraits.
As the ironclad dome of the Capitol Building
crowns the Hill,
while a lily-white brace of sanctuary angels
guarded in Corinthian Glory,
solidly stabilize
The Lily of Swampoodle.

Marble and Onyx in Main Altar

The Dome and The Light Over the Apse

Stained Glass over Main Altar

From the height of an inspired dream
Flow powers of a Tiffany-like opalescent-blue-dream that spreads
A transmundane glow
Over the altar table,
Transporting a beckoning infant
Of serenity and light
Onto all beneath.

Photos by James Sanders

Opalescent Glass Sunburst Over Sanctuary

A planetary system of circular jeweled glass,
toned according to cosmic laws of light
hovers above and central to
the radiant sanctuary.

No falling comet
can disturb the order
of the sunlit and moon-beamed pathways
or injure the harmony
of the Architect's plan
for a glazed firmament
masterly-mounted
spreading light and splendor
on all who gaze upon
the sacred treasury
beneath.

Clock Tower

Again and again upwards
free-flying birds,
expanding their wings,
in ever same migration,
rounding the ethereal clock,
the divine urge of nature,
over and again---upwards,
beyond
the City's time and boundaries.

Time wings itself free of humanity
In an uncertain course
Ready for the tasks the decades will bring,
Flowing along in a Godly procession
With insight as the Jesuits move
In place and time
Creating kaleidoscopic glory for the Lord.

Clock Photo by James Sanders

Lower Church Entrance

The Lower Church at Street Level

Surely the soundness of any structure demands a solid, firm base and the lower level of Saint Aloysius Church has been just that. Its sturdiness combined with its spaciousness has provided great flexibility through the decades with a modestly decorated area for daily masses, special interest parish activities and those of Gonzaga College. Since the establishment of the Horace McKenna S.J. Center, the daily needs of the poor and needy have expanded to the importance of its use today. Many times, when the Upper Church was not available, the Lower Church grounded all liturgies and activities to the degree that many visitors were more familiar with the warmth of the Lower Church and its role in the spiritual life of the Parish and Schools, including for many years Gonzaga, Notre Dame Academy and the Saint Aloysius Elementary School run by the Sisters of Notre Dame. As the demographics of North Capitol Street Corridor continue to change, the Lower Church area will fulfill the needs of the School and the neighborhood. In the last few years, there has been serious consideration to renovating the lower church for expanding community activities and the shelter's purposes. Decisions to move forward on any renovation of the Lower Church are underway. The needs for the expanding school facilities and the future of the neighboring community needs will figure into careful consideration for more Church expenditures.

6

Other Observations of this Place and Time

Church Front — 900 North Capitol Street

The Federal City in the Fall of 1859

The autumn-full waxing of colors
Descend across the graying City
While the folding fingers of the leaves
Let the darker seasons
Happen.

Windows in St. Al's

The Entire Church Structure

Abstracted to its basic master plan
this partly bricked, partly timbered structure
reveals itself in an elegantly simple way
yet very true to its essence.

This solidly-joined,
Inner- City-Soil connected Shepherd's tool
becomes firmly rooted in dignity
to the earth.

Windows in St. Al's

The Windows of Saint Al's
(front, side and rear)

From the outside, they are bleak
Inside they glowingly last
Like prophesies – abstract but definitely there.

At all daylight precious moments,
they become individual pictures
of rare brilliance and variegated depth.

The sides are vertical repeating squares of jewel-toned-geometrics
When in their beginnings were bright, clear, regal panes;

The inner eye catches the more elegant glass
Over the front doors,
Reminiscent of the early German Meyer Glass;
the morning light condenses itself,
assumes a softer glow
and completes itself
fulfilled in its role
as a structural picture-poem.

**Reflection on all the Architectural Details
of the Nave, the Sanctuary and Rotunda**

They flow like planetary planes and spheres
rounding about as if according
to some cosmic plan
forming without obvious pattern, a joined structural universe.

No randomly falling comet or air burst
can disturb the order
of the architect's silently calculated pathways
or destroy
the proven harmony of this Church.

Work W/C Sketch 11 by rfm

Architectural Details

The Capitals Crowning the Columns

Illustration by Nathan Leibowitz

Among the abundant bursts of branches and leaves
and marbled acanthus blossoms,
rules invisibly
the order of unity;
just as intertwined in many lives
there exits the creation
of many shapes and diversities of form.

Capital Details. Photos by J. Sanders

The Stations of the Cross

From the middle of such mission
To Calvary
Into the deadly net of human error;
While victoriously completing
His task of redemption
And bringing the reign of God,
Rising
Out of humility and mercy.

Like Him
We muster
The harsh steps
Of the Via Dolorosa.

Roman Soldier

The Putti, Angels Painted Everywhere

Young faces and figures
In a flight and dance of celestial nature
Float like day dreams
Skimming the edges and about the paintings
Spreading the order of joy by their rhythms
in hovering whimsical motions.

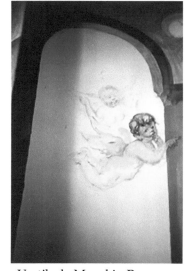

Vestibule Mural in Progress

Putti Detail by Kankanian

Brumidi Putti, Madonna Painting

Corinthyian Style Capital at Top of Cast Iron Column Supporting Main Altar

**An Expression of Gratitude to
Brumidi and Sestini, Artist and Architect**

"To Make All Things New," from *News from Eye Street*

Most of all, Constantino and Beneditto,
You have created the inner forms of your work;
You have brought to the surface
The shared meaning of your creations – a Sacred Place.
You have given shape by actually confessing,
In and outside of this structure,
Your intentions to reveal clarity to your work.

We must now see to it
To preserve that to which
You have given visible shape
By your choice of style, form and color,
To all the minute essentials to the finished work.

But especially, though, in the depths
Of your talents and dedication in hard times,
You have left us your life legacy –

The Dome over the Altar

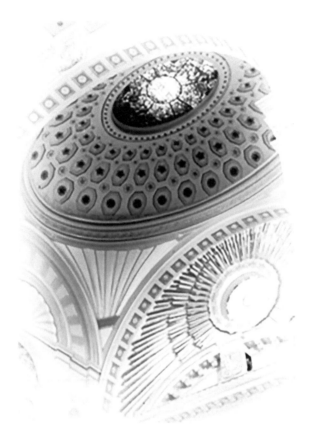

Hovering and centered,
an Infant reaches out
From the greenish-power-blues of Tiffany-like stained glass
swirling like the powers of the soul
encircling a coffered dome
above the altar.
This glowing masterpiece in sunlit glass
Reigns for always, high in sight
To the source of your strivings: God.

The Pulpit

The exploration and connection
Renovation Recap

Since 1994, the church building has been a brighter venue for liturgies, concerts and other appropriate activities. This is the result of a renovation that successfully combined the basic ingredients to "wake up" the place.

The Church is still in need of repairs and upgrades while still holding its own position in the inner-city neighborhood that holds the impressive structures of the U.S. Capitol, Supreme Court, Library of Congress and their surroundings. The population living in the adjoining streets, symmetrical in layout, pay tribute to the Fathers of our Nation while still struggling to rid some of the City's poorest housing and harassed by the "drug holes" and the stream of homeless always looking for any kind of shelter. The great complex of the Union Station, a few blocks from the Church, has created a beehive of daily workers and travelers who come and go to the sounds of the bells of Saint Aloysius and the constant resonance of traffic and soothing fountain waters splashing under thousands of homing pigeons. This is the City of Washington, D.C. Among all the marbles and granites in parks, people pass without reflecting on their meaning or their history.

Saint Aloysius is not the only historical church building on Capitol Hill. All other church structures reveal the taste and sensitivity of their builders when the City's culture was coming into being. None of the other churches structures, exactly resemble the Saint Aloysius Church building. None of the others hold the unique treasured paintings of Constantino Brumidi, the Painter of the Capitol. No other monumental church was built at the same time, with the intentions and purpose to fulfill an ideal that would support a time of a city and country while disregarding the threat of a terrible civil war waged to question, topple and change a dueling cultural system. Saint Aloysius Church has grown in reputation, deeply rooted and stabile in the City.

A Colorful Event from St. Al's early days is recounted in the following account of the wedding of the daughter of General and Mrs. Sherman

In all the active parish years of St. Aloysius Church many weddings have been performed and witnessed by all segments of Washington Society. After the 1994 Renovation, the Church became a coveted venue by brides seeking to promenade a long aisle with spacious seating for guests. One of the more famous earlier weddings occurred in October 1874, when the daughter of General and Mrs. Sherman walked down the aisle in the presence of many prominent guests. The following recounts the preparations and the event.

Invitations, issued to over 1000 read: "The General of the Army and Mrs. Sherman invite you to be present at the Nuptial Mass and Marriage of their daughter, Maria Ewing Sherman, and Thomas William Fitch, Engineer Corps, U.S.N., which will be solemnized by His Grace J.S. Purcell, Most Reverend Archbishop of Cincinnati, in St. Al's Church, Washington, DC on Thursday, October 1st, 1874, at eleven o'clock." (An invitation is preserved in St. Aloysius Archives Dr.4, Env 1). The event was generally recognized as "one of the most brilliant and impressive ceremonies ever witnessed in the National Capital." (Rev. John J. Ryan S.J., *Memoir of the Life of Rev. Richard Villager of the Society of Jesus*, Philadelphia Press of F. McManus Jr and Co., 190), p.70. Also of Star, Oct 1, 1874). Truly Ellen Sherman succeeded in her desire to show Washington how the beautiful ceremonies of a truly Catholic wedding are conducted.

Mosaic Symbol of Matrimony
in Sanctuary

Preparations began several months in advance of the big day. Minnie's wedding gown and trousseau arrived from Paris, (of rich white silk with long train trimmed with orange blossoms, the gown arrived in a six-foot long wooden box and had been packed in black oilcloth to protect it from the salt air. Burton, op.cit.). The seating arrangements for the church (admission by card only) were completed; newspapers carried front-page hints about proper dress for ladies in a Catholic church; excitement gripped the city, the parish and the Sherman household. Following a two-day steady downpour, Minnie and Will were blessed on their wedding day "with the fairest weather nature could bestow." Guests came from New England, New York, Pennsylvania and New Jersey as well as several mid-Western states. Large local crowds mobbed the streets in the vicinity of the church and home, some even climbing to the housetops in an effort to glimpse the bridal couple and the many dignitaries attending the ceremony.

Inside the edifice, its altars banked with flowers and palms, the venerable Archbishop of Cincinnati, clad in gold vestments, and displaying the jeweled symbols of his office, officiated. Assisting him were Revs. B. A. Maguire, S.J., assistant pastor at St. Aloysius, P. J. Healy, S.J., President of Georgetown College, and Thomas Mooney, the groom's Pastor from St. Bridget's Church in New York City. The prelate combined his opening instructions with recollections of his association with the Ewing family, concluding that he could not recall when a marriage ceremony has ever been performed in these United States under more interesting circumstances than the one we are assembled now to solemnize. (*Star*, October 1, 1874).

Celebrities from all branches of government added sparkle to the occasion. Heading the guest list were President and Mrs. Grant who occupied a front pew opposite the bride's family. Their unusual last-minute arrival later caused a flurry of excitement in the press, for they had met with an accident mid-way to the church and completed the journey via streetcar (*Star*, Oct.1, 1874). The horses bolted near Seventh and Kay Streets and the coachman directed them toward a nearby iron fence. As a result of the crash the White House carriage was temporarily put out of service and the Grants resorted to public transportation as the most expeditious mean available). General Philip Sheridan rushed from Chicago for the ceremony (so hastily did the General don his uniform after arriving in Washington and dash to the church, that one observer termed it, "Sheridan's second ride." Burton, op.cit. p.222.) and joined other military guests, all resplendent in full-dress uniform. Supreme Court Justices and members of the Diplomatic Corps filled the front pews of the side aisles. That evening, thanks to a local balladeer, Washington citizens would have a better idea of exactly who had jammed the church earlier in the day:

> And Grant was there, and Phil was there
> And all the soldiers in town were there;
> The ladies were there, bedad they were,
> and all had flowers in their hair.

The Priests stood by, all robed and serene
And the grandest Archbishop that ever was seen;
The Pope he wrote that he would have come
But important business kept him home.

(Quoted in Durkin op.cit., p13.)

Following the lengthy religious ceremony, guests proceeded immediately to the Sherman home for a breakfast and reception. Here again they could see evidence of the detailed attention given to the entire event, for the bridal couple stood under an elaborate custom-designed wedding bell which came from Boston. Over 1000 persons filed by to wish them happiness while outside the Army band played appropriate songs.

Despite the lengthy press reports which detailed the nuptials, it did not escape attention that this was also the Sherman's farewell to Washington. Reporters lauded the General for his military accomplishments. Some voiced the hope that he might return as President. One editor focused his column on the distaff side of the family, stating that with Mrs. Sherman's departure the poor will lose one of their best friends, the young their most thoughtful patroness and society one of its most exemplary members. (9Cf. Burton, op.cit.,pp 222-23 for unidentified quotations.) A short time later, the entire family journeyed West to St. Louis. They left an indelible mark, especially on St. Aloysius' Parish, for during their short residency they had been among its most active supporters and workers.

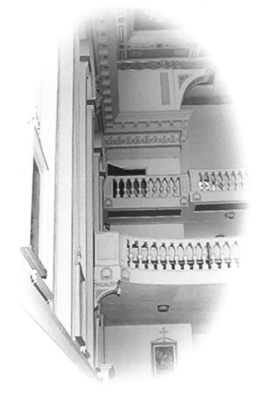

Two Tribunes

Damage Control and Overview

Décor Inset in Arch   1859 Remnants of Original Ceiling Décor

The reason for the 1993/4 Renovation was the Church became dangerous to use. The ceiling materials began to fall away. Dampness from continuing leaking walls and roof caused mildew and weakness in the structure. The Brumidi paintings were beginning to show many decades of neglect and a decline in the integrity of the canvases and pigments.

There were two solutions for the building. Complete Restoration or a careful renovation. Renovation was the option owing to the limited amount of money available and the more obvious damages could be addressed by a careful renovation. In 1993, a call for bids was made. Three contractors replied and one, Ferrandi Associates from Baltimore, was chosen on the basis of costs and their impressive visual presentation of their design proposals. The real work began in the summer of 1993 with demolition and the scaffolding put in place to work on the higher wall elevations and ceiling.

Ceiling Panel Removed

Terry Matan, John Warman, Steve Ferrandi and Murray Observing
Original 10' x 10' Ceiling Panel

Watercolor by Murray

"The Two Trinities," Detail

The fine art conservation company chosen to work on three Brumidi paintings was Page Conservation Inc., Washington, D.C. Arthur Page had the large altar painting and the two circular tondos removed to his conservatory. The photos shown here are those taken by Page during the restoration of the paintings.

The large altar painting began to show evidence of bubbling in 2011. Recently, a team from the Office of the Architect of the Capitol came down to St. Al's and donated their time and services to solving the canvas's bubbling problem.

Although the actual monetary value of the Brumidi works has never been fixed, we know that they are invaluable as works of art by the Italian Immigrant Artist, Constantino Brumidi, who gained international notoriety for his work in the U.S. Capitol. If these paintings were seriously damaged or lost entirely, the cost to have a master painter recreate them would be in the upper six figures or more.

The remaining two Brumidi paintings, "The Flight into Egypt" (a.k.a. "The Two Trinities") and the "Madonna of Sorrows" were removed to an upper room in the Gonzaga Complex where they were cleaned and received a modicum of inpainting and repair by Armen Kankanian, the Armenian Artist and Architect who created the murals in the vestibule niches. In addition, Armen carefully cleaned the 14 canvases depicting the Passion of Christ. The canvases themselves received no additional inpainting.

In 1994, Armen carefully applied a neutral-toned finish on both the statues of St. Francis and St. Ignatius. Now, both of these representations are in need of attention and new considerations will be given to improving their pedestals.

St. Francis Xavier, S.J.

Ignatious Loyola, Founder of
The Society of Jesus

Thinking Back and Through the Art

We have here a church structure, built of brick in mid-19th century America by the Jesuits. The architecture is of European Renaissance influence; the Architect was an emigrant Jesuit priest from Italy; the artists seen in the interior were Italians; one an emigrant form Armenia. The imposition of this structure and the art it represents into the Federal City of Washington brought a heavy influential example from Old World culture to the New World. This church building was not the first one of its type of architecture in America, but it was one that had significant influence on the architects and city planners of Washington at that critical developing time of the City.

Saint Aloysius Church speaks to the power and freedom of art that emerged from the influences of the Renaissance. Its strong devotional theme brought the allegorical, the intellectual and a spiritual freedom that was driving, by the 19th century, artistic function in residential, commercial and sacred structure building in Europe and America. The artistic fantasies of bringing to the forefront the classical art of Rome and Athens were fulfilled after a long dark cultural period. It was to last until today although being moderated now by other developing building materials and advancing ideas for their use. In fact, Saint Aloysius Church appears to be fading in its earlier prominence from being recognized as a Washington landmark of its own kind.

The highly stylized classical paintings inside borrow much from Renaissance painters in technique qualities and in the manner they depicted religious and biblical scenes. They imposed on society visuals that were unreal in actuality, but brilliantly rendered or painted in very pleasing manners. They inserted the ornamental, the fashionable and non-relevant to the theme, objects to fill out huge canvases and in undertaking monumental reproductions of famous devotional scenes or themes. These artists, like Brumidi and Gagliardi, wanted to place power and authority into their works. Either they wanted to make themselves better known to the influential or they needed to hide some realities (like the Way of the Cross paintings) with fashionable or comedic figures. It was well known that some of the great earlier Italian painters like Caravaggio, searched the back streets of Rome for models in their greatest devotional paintings ("Christ at Emmaeus," now in Vienna) to bring stronger impact and maybe controversy to himself. Like Caravaggio, whose soiled personal life on the back streets

Drawing by Nathan Leibowitz

Photo composition "From Back to Front "
by J. Sanders

of Rome followed his reputation, other great painters merged into world of art despite their questionable personal exploitations.

The lives of Brumidi and Gagliardi, for what is known, had their own challenges in life, but in their efforts to paint pleasing personages there is remarkable evidence of pathos and understanding for the human condition that appears, particularly in the individual portrayals seen in the Way of the Cross where the suffering, horror and trauma of crucifixion is expressed in oil on the faces of the onlookers or traditional depictions of those directly involved with the totality of the happening situation. Outrage is seen, trauma captured, harmony shattered by death. Artistically executed, in a very orderly and pleasing manner, all Renaissance artists made beauty from chaos. The ugly transformed to the appealing.

Our paintings in Saint Aloysius Church, in their own way, are utopian visions of balance i.e., how the situations and settings and everything in the world can be brought into the harmony of aesthetic expression. The artist brings his own style or quality of imagination into his own conception of reality. We call it his own composition brought into the limits and scope of the medium and ground on which he chooses to create his work. When Brumidi offers his own depiction of the Communion of Aloysius in his elaborate home, he depicts the boy in a mild state of rapture about what is taking place. This expression is Brumidi's choice or feeling about what the situation could have been. In turn, Brumidi offers us our own choice of accepting his vision or choosing to make or reject what may be our own conception of the event. This scenario is what contributes thought and variable meanings to the world of art. Certainly, Brumidi perceives this event in Aloysius's life as the fulcrum to the integrity and stability of his youth and the meaningfulness of his name as patron of this church.

Reflections of Brumidi's life as an immigrant to America pave a way to a question how much his immigrant status contributed to the vulnerability of his kind of painting in the eyes of his critics. They could see dignity and clarity in his compositions; they found symbols of the American Frontier and earlier markings of the New World; they determined how he saw the progress of the American Spirit from boundary to boundary and its integration as the two coasts were joined together in union of purpose. His overwhelming power and authority as a productive artist for twenty-five continuous years, sweeps through the walls and ceilings and corridors of

Pulpit and Painting

the entire Capitol Building. Did his critics lock onto the liberating force and dedicated efforts Brumidi and all artists create when given the freedom and resources to do the work they envision?

There were critics who felt that Brumidi, the immigrant, was allowed too much leeway to produce classical and thought-to-be European-imagery for Americans. History of the time shows a lot of effort to bring him down from his scaffolding and future eminent standing as the Artist of the U.S. Capitol. He persisted, however, and kept on painting and often for little remuneration, because he knew in his heart that he had to express his sentiments of being a true, grateful "American" from his draft renderings to the tip of his brushes. It is documented also, that Brumidi was willing to work for far less money than any other capable artist of his time. Often, he was modestly paid from project to project and had to wait for available funds to proceed in his overall painting schedule. This was a very practical decision for an artist of his caliber to make. Pre-Civil War money was becoming scarce, especially for matters and project of the Public Fine Arts. The Arts and Cultural pursuits rarely thrive in seasons of war talk rumors.

Today's Renaissance-type painting followers bring humanism combined with elegance in life and beauty. Sometimes these "old" paintings seem naive and unrealistic and overdone to the point of absurdity. Nevertheless, they belong to history and are culturally important. We may presume they are spiritually motivated and have been objects of sincere devotion for over 150 years. We cannot know how they will be criticized in the future or if they will be here to see. This writing gives testament to what we see here now.

Work Pause

Church Building, Its Roles in the Future

It is a developing story that brings some certainties. In the future, church architects will use not only conventional building materials but other newer materials to provide thoughtful ways of expression. Builders and architects over the past decades have brought into play materials that convey fresher ideas and ways of community worship and services. We see completely new and different ways to assemble and pray in a world of increasing technical progress.

Places of prayer are becoming simpler in design with less attention to extravagance to more focus and flexibility creating more attention to the substance of spirituality, i.e. to a real understanding and connection to the God.

Ceiling Medallion

Instead of large spaces with stiff, crowded pews, once garnered with gilt and ornamentation, more practical space configurations with mobile furnishings will appear for easy handling and reasonable comfort. The emphasis will be put upon the liturgies and services. There will always be a place for relevant works of fine art and a contemporary-styled décor that carries a spiritual message.

The emphasis of architecture today is upon the use of light and more advanced durable materials. It is the proper use and realization of space that gives dignity to any place, situation or thought.

Sestini's overall achievement created a sense of space and utility on a rather small piece of city property. His use of a combination of styles did not go overboard or muddy the design. St. Al's architecture has been often termed incorrectly as Renaissance, Gothic and even Baroque. Actually, its style is mostly of the simpler Romanesque style with some decorative elements of other related artistic motifs. You can tell by the photographs over the years that the church sanctuary has become more simplified and useful through its litany of renovations. The exterior building has kept the same simple, clean appearance since its founding.

Saint Aloysius was designed for church and community events and will continue to play its historical role of influence to the architectural life of the City of Washington, D.C.

Working Correspondence

Letters from Bob Thuman, the Church Decorative Artist, and Frank Duane, the Renovation Overseeing Architect, where each recount the scope and descriptions of their work.

Working Watercolor Sketch by Murray

April 24, 2011

Robert F. Murray, Renovation Aesthetics Director
The von Brahler Ltd. Art Presentation and Consultations
c/o Saint Aloysius Church Office, Washington, D.C.

Dear Bob:

It was good to hear from you. I also think about you and at times the other members of your 1994 restoration committee. I had been back one or two times to touch up some water-damaged areas.

Watercolor Sketch by Murray

There is something that I have seen that is very disturbing to me. Decisions by pastors who want to brighten up a church by hiring painters at a low price who quickly spray paint everything regardless of the decorative values. I had applied 3" wide band of 23K gold leaf inside the coffered ceiling panels in the sanctuary of a church in Baltimore during the 1970's. The church is close to where I lived, and I would occasionally attend services or concerts there. When I had applied the gold leaf, the cost of the material was probably around $1500 then. In 2009, I attended a service there and saw that some painters had very quickly applied a coat of paint to this entire ceiling and then applied a cheap "gold" paint where I had applied the gold leaf. At St. Aloysius back in 1994 my purchase of the gold leaf was about $10,000. I believe the value of gold at that time was $400/ounce.
I hope these thoughts of mine will be helpful to you in your quest to maintain the integrity of your beautiful St. Aloysius.

Sincerely.
Robert S. Thuman

Post Scriptum

1. I first worked on the 1959 Church Project as a 28-year-old for William A. Octavec and Sons who were in a loose partnership with T.J. Gibbons. In 1991-4 restoration, Robert S. Thuman and Son did the gold leaf work and the decorative painting.
2. I was impressed by the renovation committee, their knowledge and judgment.
3. I retouched some of the water-damaged areas in the Church in 1959 and again in 2005 and 2006.
4. It was such a pleasure working with you, Fr. Dooley, Frank Duane, John Delaney, Stu Long and Terry Matan and all day-workers and team and experience your enthusiasm and dedications to this long-needed project.
5. Hold onto this signature Washington landmark building as long as you can.

Bob, I have since retired and turned over my business to my son whom you will remember worked with me at Saint Al's. Pray for me. RT

Extensive Scaffolding

Recap of '94 Renovation by Frank Duane, Overseeing Architect

Robert F. Murray
Swampoodle Lily, Author and Editor
Alexandria, Va. 22306

RE: St. Aloysius Church Interior Church Restoration Project, Washington, D.C.

Pursuant to your request, I have enumerated my recollection of what we accomplished during 1993 and 1994 on the subject project, along with Rev. Bernard J. Dooley SJ and his handpicked executive committee. I was pleased to be honored and selected to advise the committee and help direct the proposed restoration work in The Great Church of St. Aloysius. My selection as architect was probably related to other church and restoration work in the metro area and my long-term affiliations with Gonzaga after my promotion in to the real world, Class of 1950.

The following is a brief resume of the pertinent issues we addressed and accomplished, and of course is subject to your poetic license, and Terri's and Stu's review and comments.

The initial goal of the endeavor was to salvage the interior from long term and advancing deterioration, related to age, required maintenance, and overdue restoration. The project was basically limited to interior work only, due to our budget limitations. Necessary exterior work was pushed to the future, i.e., masonry, windows, roofing, organ repair, tower, etc.

The original project scope was limited to nave repairs and new finishes, sanctuary liturgical changes, painting's preservation, required HVAC work, lighting, and pew work and was expanded during progress as other priorities developed.

Altar Angel

ORGANIZATION

Prior to my selection, Father Bernie Dooley, S.J., (long term President of Gonzaga high school) had organized a large committee of qualified persons to assist him in initiation of the project. The poor condition of the Brumidi paintings in the sanctuary and on the proscenium walls was one of the major factors in planning the restoration project. I did advise Father that in order to expedite the decision making and direct the work during construction, that we needed to have a small executive group to effectively review and manage what we could accomplish with available funds, within the allocated time frame. His selection of the group included, Mrs. Terri Matan, Stuart Long Esq, Robert F. Murray, and Frank Duane AIA and we met weekly on site with Bernie to manage the project and negotiate priorities. Terri's stately presence and advice assured some decorum and prevented unruly, unacceptable male behavior during the construction period (approx. 7 months). We all got the opportunity to give "hands-on" gold leafing touches to the wall frieze surrounding the nave.

DESIGN OBJECTIVES

Restore the interior of the building and return it to its past prominence and use as a historic religious, civic, community, and educational facility. My vision, as architect, was to create a church interior which projected, a highly visible religious space emphasized by and thru the elongated nave, up to the altered sanctuary area, and provide a temperature-controlled environment to permit its use for multiple purposes, and provide for preservation of the art work and interior.

Ashley Hawken Talking with Frank Duane Architect

RESEARCH

Preliminary research was initiated, but no architectural drawings by Rev. Benedict Sestini, S.J., the original 1860 era architect, were obtainable or discovered. No other useable drawing information or data was found in the church's records. Since we were fast-tracking the schedule, we produced field sketches and drawings to outline the various work areas along with details and specs as necessary to prepare bid packages, to obtain proposals on the architectural portions of the work.

BUDGET

The cost of the project was developed by the exec. group by obtaining competitive quality-based proposals and was controlled by Fr. Dooley. We periodically pleaded with Bernie for budget adjustment, up or down, based on priorities. Bernie, whom we all knew as personal friends, was a universally acclaimed soft-sell fund raiser, and was somewhat reticent to share the changing status of the budget and or donors, but would always come up with funding for urgent needs, i.e., narthex flooring costs. Based on memory, the approx. construction costs on the project, in round numbers, by contracts, was as follows:

Restoration work	700,000
Heating, ventilating, and air conditioning	460,000
Electric power distribution system	30,000
New lighting systems	donated
Painting restoration work	100,000
Permits, printing, mechanical engineering, miscel. soft costs	20,000
Sound system	30,000
Marble flooring, stone work, altar	donated
Sanctuary furniture	4,000

IMPLEMENTATION

After the initial planning and bid, phase work was completed in 1993, the upper church was closed in early 1993. The exec. committee effected a modified CM (construction management) procedure to accomplish the project and control the time frame and costs. As we advanced into the work, my involvement included advice, architectural services, construction observation, and part time project management services...the AE team included, Ed Beall PE (Class of '43) mechanical engineer, Edward J. Scullen, structural engineer, Frank Gleeson, electrical contractor (Class of '50), Gallery owner Robert F. Murray (Class of '53), provided the artistic overview necessary for the selection and observation of the paintings restorer. Through preparation of quality and cost-based proposals, we obtained competitive proposals from three contractors, who were then interviewed.

We selected the following:

A. Steve Ferrandi, a Baltimore based, father-son, church restoration contractor to provide: demolition, painting, wall covering, carpentry, millwork, plastering, pew refinishing and labor;.

B. Murray Mechanical (not related to Bob Murray, the author) to complete the heating, ventilating and air conditioning systems.

Through direct negotiation, we selected the following:

A. Gleason Electric Co. to install new power and electric systems including custom lighting design systems; B. R. Braddi & Son for the marble, tile and stone work.

SCOPE OF WORK

Architecturally speaking we accomplished the interior restoration program and environmental changes by designing, implementing, and coordinating the following to enhance, and improve the character, appearance and functions of the facility by:

A. Opening the enclosed narthex into the nave to improve the entrance area and visibility of the sanctuary.

Photo of Altar Scaffolding by James Sanders

Removal of communion rail

B. Making currently required liturgical changes in the sanctuary area.

C. Changing the color schemes and finishes to enhance the appearance of the interior spaces.

D. Designing new lighting and power systems for the church and rectory and providing lighting of the nave, sanctuary, and art work which demonstrate their architectural character.

E. Providing new esthetically integrated environmental HVAC systems, meeting current ASHRAE and code standards.

F. Removal and restoration, off site, and re-installation of the Brumidi paintings.

G. Required repair, and or, new work on the monumental exterior front entry stairs and in the sacristy, and roofing.

H. Selective demolition and removal of over 100 years of debris from the church attic.

HISTORIC ITEMS

Jesuit Miracle: During progress of the work, a homeless McKenna center visitor, who was hired as a laborer by the contractor, fell approx. 80 feet from the top level of the ceiling scaffolding and was seriously injured. During his medical operations and rehabilitation, he was visited frequently by members of the Jesuit community and was returned to an active lifestyle.

One of the historic items discovered below the wood floor was a church bulletin from the early nineteen hundreds which outlined the proposed electrification of the church which was to be funded by parishioners, whose family names are still recognized today.

During attic investigations (since no architectural info was available from the church), I discovered that the main roof framing (trusses) were constructed from solid redwood timbers, most likely shipped from California in the 1860 period.

Franklin J. Duane-Architect

Post scriptum—Sometime after opening of the church, Bernie did show me a set of measured drawings (approx. size was 14 by 20) of St. Aloysius prepared by Maguire and Maguire, Architects from NYC dated in 1939. One of the Maguire's is in north Naples and a neighbor of my close friend Vince Murphy. Bernie said that he got them from Gonzaga archives. I didn't get them copied since work was over and we suffered thru without them. They should be very helpful if you can retrieve them. I also have some excellent interior photos of the completed interior taken by Don Savage, my principle sidekick at DCMM, which I can get copied for you. Let me know what all you would like me to do. Haven't typed this much since US Army days in 1956. Also from a historic point, my brother-in-law's deceased uncle was Brumidi's lawyer who settled his estate. He had one of Brumidi's drawings which I think my brother-in-law gave to Bernie. I can verify this if you wish. (This gift is the oil sketch by Brumidi of "The Assumption of Our Lady," now in the Students Chapel, Gonzaga College High School).

Oil Sketch by Brumidi of Mary, St. Francis, St. Roche with Dog, now in
Gonzaga Student's Chapel

"Lily Grows in Sunlight," Photo by James Sanders

Interior Stairwell

Working Watercolor Sketch by Murray

Reviving the Lily of 900 North Capitol Street

Anatomy of Renovation, Saint Aloysius Gonzaga Church, Washington, DC
By, Bob Murray, Renovation Co-Chair

DETERIORATION (1991)

Awareness
Need
Dialogue
Planning Committee Formation
Review, Past, Present, and Future Use
Overseeing Architect's Appointment
Dialogue
Vision
Planning the Dream
Invitation to Contractors
Budget Considerations
Fund Raising
Contract Proposals
Review of Presentations
Dialogue
Revision of the Dream
Review of Available Archival Materials
City Permit Applications
Award of Contract
Dialogue
Working Committee Formation

DEMOLITION (1993)

Daily Review of Work Orders
Hiring of Labor
Detail of Architect's Blueprints
Sizing and Ordering of New Marble Flooring
Construct of Sub-Flooring
Committee Dialogue
Church Décor Painter Plan
Color Palette Choices Review and Testing Samples
Review of Budget and Revision of Plans

Review, Removal and Check on Conservator of Major Oil Paintings
Review of Electrical and A/C Installations
Prep of Walls for New Frescos
Preview Plan to Reopening and Architect's Assessments of Contractors'
    Compliances
Installation of New Marble and Return of Major Paintings/Tweeking and
Corrections to Church Painting Décor to Walls and Ceiling
Final Review of Contract Performance and Amendments

REOPENING CEREMONY (1994)

Lily Revived
Creation of Committee for the Use, Care and Preservation of the Church
    Building

Renewal

The Game of Floaters

Remember the game "Interlock your fingers and say here is the church, here is the steeple, open the doors (your hands) and see all the people?" If you take down the church, you take out the people. What is left? A ruin? A memory? A piece of land? An old idea of what the church represented at one time? A spirituality left to wander around the neighborhood like a lost dog begging for a home? I'm not certain what is left when an historical meaningful church is erased from the ground. It is sad, at the least. The Washington Post of January 4, 2014, ran an article about the fate of the red sandstone Gothic styled, twin-spired, Trinity Episcopal church, designed by the New York architect, James Renwick, that stood at the northeast corner of Third and C Streets, N.W., Washington, DC. It went into use May 1851 and was demolished in 1936 to make space for a fourteen thousand square foot parking lot. The article by John Kelly quotes, "many venerable parishioners have raised Cain, to quote one church official, about the demolition of the old edifice. They've termed the destruction of the landmark a sacrilege, heartless and commercial decision." But, a temple which doesn't pay must fall. And so, fall they do, the old church landmarks in America and around the globe. Some just fall down from pure neglect; others fall down under the pressure of some other idea. The parishioners are attracted to another more desirable location in an area or are pressured out by decisions closed to explanation to the general public.

Trinity Episcopal Church was just nine years older than Saint Aloysius Church that opened in 1859. Both churches experienced their wealthiest church members moving to the more attractive parts of the northwest sector of Washington. The neighborhood around the Capitol had become occupied by "a floating population." So far, Saint Aloysius Church has weathered the demographic changes as well as the wear of the seasons' elements. However, a newly floating population is flowing back into its neighborhood and we are expecting a new demand for old Saint Aloysius Church to be of its original intended service to the inner city of Washington.

So, let's play that game again, "There is the church, there is the steeple, open the door and see all the new people." This book will tell and show what the people will see – that which has been preserved and cared for, and why.

"St. Al's Structure—Stabile, Preserved and Dignified," by Murray

St. Al's, Stabilized and Dignified

A church structure is a stage for spirituality. The stage, by its purpose, is the platform where the players act, the place for spiritual expression and experience. In the history of sacred places, the "church place" grew from a designated revered spot to a manmade structure. Elaborate or plain, the design or architecture must speak for itself.

Church architecture critics praise or condemn classical and modern designs. Their opinions depend on an educated or spiritual experience coupled, perhaps, with a knowledge or past interaction with some particular style of church place. Often a person feels a kind of personality deaden-

The Former Eye Street, NW, Renewed

ing in a location or building. On the other hand, architecture like art can lighten the mind. Glazed and naturally lighted, angular or rather business-like spaces clear the mind and spirit. The subdued, stained glass prismatic glows in a vertical and art- filled space can coax elevated feelings and awe. The effect of the architecture works both ways – it is what it brings to you and what you bring to it.

The Saint Aloysius Church is obviously traditional. About twenty+ years ago, the renovation working committee intentionally attempted to simplify (contemporize) the interior by eliminating some of the ornate decorative oil painting in the sanctuary and altar areas. Neutral tones of paint were applied to the walls and lightly trimmed with a blue tone and a minimum of gold leaf accent. The plan was to bring the eye onto more of a focus to the central Brumidi altarpiece painting. The marble floor of the sanctuary itself was extended twenty-six feet into the nave to bring the action of the liturgy and other appropriate events closer to the audience.

Saint Aloysius's open, rectangular space houses an appropriate use of li-turgical painting and sculpture to represent its Jesuit mission to the in-ner city of Washington. The actual size of the interior, although appearing grand, has never been thought to be oversized for its usage. If anything, it

Side Altar Marble Relief

has been too small in recent years for some academic-related events. The church is located within the same city block on the campus of the Gonzaga College High School where young men, since 1821, have been educated to find God in all people, situations and things.

In the '60's and '70's, a confluence of church designers brought to the business of church design the idea to sideline the tabernacle which contains the Eucharist to a side altar or rear of the church. Traditionally in our church, the tabernacle was the centerpiece of the main altar. We hope that the present home of the Eucharist in a side altar will be returned to its pivotal position under the main altar painting.This will bring the return of the once more prominently suspended Sanctuary Lamp.

Light of the Inner City, always welcoming the young to the Lily of Spirit,
Carrying the inspiration and images of this place, where generations
Stepped to this stage, this nave, this sanctuary, this vessel of hope,
dignity and stability
In the home voyage to a vanishing future.

Side Altar Marble Relief

A Vanishing Point

The roads we often travel
Appear too dark.
They are thick with trees
blocking our way.

But sometimes in that darkness
we find our way to the door of an uncommon place
brighter and safer.

A church is a neutral spot, a finding place,
Away but not divorced from earthly reality.
It is a clear, silent space
calming noise and nerves
In the City.

This sacred space
erases confusion and gloom,
by creating a connection
for the soul
to ride in the wake
of the invisible Being,
that vanishes into
a new light,
only to return
sometime in the reign and realm of God's own logic.

N. Capitol Street, NW

In Conclusion

I believe the newest generations of architects will envision the unexplored and the imaginative in building and decor. They will advance sound and musical capabilities, fresh design concepts and greater challenges in urban and rural locations. Our traditional Saint Aloysius Church will take its classical bow to an expanding, more modern City of Washington. Any substitute structure for our present church structure will have a resemblance of design that can be recognized as a Jesuit Style. As long as the Jesuits maintain their role in this City and Nation, there will emerge a new Sestini with a new Brumidi to give the future Saint Aloysius Church an innate sense of its own Jesuit Rhythm.

Now and in recent decades, we are blessed and grateful for Pastors and Gonzaga Presidents who have taken great care of Saint Aloysius. The existing members of the Committee for the Preservation, Care and Use of the Church Building, formed by the Alumni President, John J. Delany '50, encourage the concerns for the future of the church among the Gonzaga Board of Directors, the Faculty and Students and each Gonzaga Family Association especially the watchful eyes of the Gonzaga Alumni Association.

Ad Majorem Dei Gloriam

Portrait of St. Aloysius by Leonid Bodnia (Uzbekistan)

Post Scriptum: The landmark building, Saint Aloysius Church, could have been built in Swampoodle only by great men like Sestini and Brumidi with vision to provide a sacred place with the integrity, dignity and stability necessary for the Jesuits' roles in serving the parish and in the education of Gonzaga boys. I am one of those boys who came over the Potomac on a Capital Transit streetcar that wound through Georgetown, over Pennsylvania Ave, up Mass. Avenue and turned onto North Capitol Street to Swampoodle where I trudged happily with an unknown future, up the purple alley beneath the clock aside the church built and designed by a Jesuit priest carrying his faded green umbrella. I tried to follow, in some measures of my own, in his artistic footsteps, inspiration and overall concerns for the future of St. Al's.

As it was once prayerfully said in those earlier Gonzaga days,

> *Ad introibo Ad altari Dei, ad Deum qui laetificat*
> *ad jeuventutem meum, i.e., I will go to the altar of God,*
> *to God who gives joy to my youth.*

> (Missale Romanum)

Gonzaga Graduates in foreground of St Al's

Author's experiences on exploring printed matter archival resources: Many of the mentions of historical and archival details came from unmarked sources discovered in the Gonzaga and St. Aloysius Church Archives which had been moved in recent years from their original locations to another venue. For one reason or another, many materials appear to have been separated from their originally marked placements. The same situation was discovered in the many boxes of related but randomly-placed materials found in the Georgetown University Archives, many of which were very fragile to physically handle. This often found situation is what contributes to the difficulties, long times and expenses in researching factual histories of any kind.

Not many years ago, I chaired a search committee to find the appropriate author to compile a written history of Gonzaga to commemorate its 200th anniversary in 2021. After a significant time and interviewing three prospective authors, it was determined that the ordering of the Gonzaga Archives themselves would consume so much time and resources that would have to be expended before any author could seriously and practically consider doing any comprehensive history. When and if an "archives project" would be undertaken, it was determined that compiling a written history would take the appointed author at least three more years to complete. The written history project was tabled for further consideration at that time. My compilation of visuals and text about St. Aloysius Church's points of interest is a much lesser effort than what will be needed to research all the history and details of a comprehensive written history of Gonzaga College High School, Saint Aloysius Church and the times of the Saint Aloysius Parish. I suspect that any future historical effort elaborating on the entire Gonzaga Complex on Eye Street will come in the form of whatever visual method is expedient at that time. Someday a full recounting of the closely-related histories of the School, Church and Parish will reveal the fuller flowering of the Swampoodle Lily.

"About Town," *Washington Post,* 1994

Swampoodle Lilies Mosaic of Altar Pedestal

The Chalice of Dignity, Integrity, and Stability of Youth,
Photo by James Sanders

Overview of Church During Funeral Mass for Stuart Long, 1960,
Outstanding Gonzaga Graduate and Major Benefactor to both Gonzaga and
St. Aloysius' Church.

Appendix 1

B.C. into A.D.

The following dates and architectural accomplishments are selected at random to emphasize the progression of architecture in our world, with particular emphasis on the sacred places, places and temples of worship.

Circa 10000 B.C.
Primitive man comes out of caves and forests and begins to construct rough shelters from a variety of plant and animal products.

Circa 5000 B.C.
Megaliths and dolmens still stand today that are remnants of earthen mounds revealing standing stones. Isolated stone structures also appear.

Circa 3200 – 2859 B.C.
The White Temple of Warka is built – the base of which is the earliest type of Babylonian ziggurat. Samarian temples come about in Lower Mesopotamia. The phenomenon of "writing and drawing" makes its debut.

Circa 3000 B.C.
Mastaba-style Egyptian tombs with flat roofs were built. In 2778 B.C., the world's first largest monument in stone – the Step Pyramid of Zoser were built by Cheops at Sakkara. In 2723-2563 B.C., from Egypt's oldest kingdom came the Great Pyramid of Giza; the second pyramid and the Sphinx at Giza was put up by Chephren and, later, Mycerinus built the third and last pyramid.

Circa 1520 B.C.
At Thebes, the Mortuary Temple of Hatshepsut was constructed. Around 605 to 563, Babylon was rebuilt by Nebuchadnezzar II and the hanging Gardens and Ishtar Gate are built.

Circa 447-425 B.C.
The best example of Greek architecture, The Parthenon, goes up on the Athens Acropolis and the Temple of Athena Nike was added to the Acropolis as well as The Erechtheum.

312 B.C.
The Via Appia, uniting Rome to the south of Italia, was begun by the Romans; the first aqueduct is also underway to completion.

214 B.C.
The Great Wall of China is finished.

82 – 79 B.C.
The Sanctuary of Fortuna Primigenia was built by the Romans at Palestrina. And around 54 B.C. Julius Caesar glorifies Rome with a larger Forum – a precedent followed by Augustus, Vespasian, Nerva and Emperor Trajan. Julius Caesar was murdered in 44 B.C.

11 B.C.
A temple, built as the precursor of the Pantheon, by Agrippa, was damaged by fire in the first century A.D.

4 A.D.
The Birth of Jesus Christ
.

70-82 A.D.
The Colloseum, begun by Vespasian, was finished by Domitian.

120 A.D.
The gem of Roman style, the Pantheon, was reconstructed by Hadrian.

312 A.D.
Constantine orders built the great triumphal arch in Rome as the symbol of his victory over Maxentius.

300 A.D.
The first basilicas began to appear in Rome. In 532-37, the Hagia Sophia was rebuilt by Justinian and is considered "the" monument of Byzantine style.

607 A.D.
Horyuji Monastery went up in Nara, Japan – the Golden Hall remains the oldest wooden building in existence.

625 A.D.–786 A.D.
Mohammed founds the first Islamic mosque in Medina. In 786, the masterpiece of Islamic architecture, Cordoba's Great Mosque was begun by Abd-al-Rahman.

804 A.D.
Palatine Chapel at Aachen was finished by Charlemagne.

900 A.D.
Great Buddhist Temple of Borobudur appeared in Indonesia.

960 A.D.
In London, Westminster Abbey's predecessor, The Benedictine Abbey, appeared.

1000 A.D.
The magnificent Great Temple at Bhuvaneshwar, Hindu temple was constructed in India.

1137-44 A.D.
The first Gothic structure was built by Abbe Sugar, -Abbey Church of Saint Denis.

1160-1290 A.D.
Lyon Cathedral was built. 1163-1250, Notre Dame de Paris appears; Soissons Cathedral was built; 1194-1260, the Cathedral of Chartres went up. Reims Cathedral was built from 1211 to 1290. Cologne Gothic Cathedral was begun in 1248.

1200 A.D.–1204 A.D.
Cambodia saw the great Angkor Wat temple arise. In 1204, Hagia Sophia was damaged in Constantinople by Crusaders

1420-1434 A.D.
Brunelleschi's dome caps the Florence Duomo – a blend of a Renaissance dome with a Gothic building. From 1421-45 in Florence, the Foundling Hospital was erected – a Renaissance style edifice.

1429-46 A.D.
Brunelleschi built Pazzi Chapel in Florence.

1506-1546 A.D.
St. Peter's Basilica was erected in Rome; the dome was designed by Michelangelo. Michelangelo also designed a third story for the Farnese Palace, begun by Antonio da Sangallo the Younger in 1546.

1536-53 A.D.
The Library of St. Mark was built in Venice by Jacopo Sansovino.

1546-1878 A.D.
A total history of the French Renaissance became manifest by the building of the Louvre in Paris.

1570 A.D.
The "Four Books of Architecture" by Andrea Palladio, became the greatest influence on architectural designs throughout Renaissance Europe.

1630 – 1653 A.D.
The Taj Mahal in Agra became India's jewel.

1661 A.D.
Versailles was started by Louis XIV of neoclassical style.

1675-1710 A.D.
St. Paul's Church by Sir Christopher Wren, in London replaced an earlier cathedral destroyed in the Great Fire.

1696 – 1720 A.D.
The Hapsburg residence in Vienna was modeled after Versailles. Blenheim Palace in England became a fine example of Baroque style.

1792 A.D.
The President's House for Washington was designed by James Hoban in the English Palladian Style architecture.

1815 – 1829 A.D.
The United States Capitol, begun in Palladian lines by William Thornton, was rebuilt by Latrobe and Bullfinch after the War of 1812.

1823- 1860 A.D.
In London, Robert Smirke built the Greek Revival, British Museum. Later, the Houses of Parliament of Gothic origin/style.

1857 A.D.
The important Elisha Graves Otis first passenger safety elevator went into a New York Department Store.

1905 – 1910 A.D.
Antol Gaudi built the Casa Mila in Barcelona.

1911-1913 A.D.
Le Corbusier erected his famous house, Villa Les Terraces at Garches, France.

1930 – 1939 A.D.
Empire State Building, New York City. In 1939, marked the completion of the Rockefeller Center.

1936 – 1949 A.D.
Frank Lloyd Wright built Falling Water in Pennsylvania and the Johnson Wax Company in Wisconsin.

1946-1959 A.D.
Le Corbusier built the Unites d'Habitation in Marseille, the "vertical city." The United Nation's Headquarters went up in New York under a team of architects including Le Corbusier, Wallace Harrison, Oscar Niemeyer and

Sven Markelius. The Lever House was built on Park Avenue in 1952 in New York. In 1959, Frank Lloyd Wright built the Solomon R. Guggenheim Museum.

1968 A.D.
The Lincoln Center for the Performing Arts was finished 1968.

1973 A.D.
The World Trade Center's twin towers were finished and Australia's Sydney Opera Center opened as well as the Sear Towers in Chicago.

More contemporary architecture to follow in the future.

Appendix 2

A small list of Brumidi's works

There is an unending list of works in the Capitol, the most prominent being "The Apotheosis" covering the central rotunda.

"The Apotheosis of Washington" (1865).

Fresco on the Canopy of the U.S. Capitol's Rotunda.
Photo Courtesy Architect of the Capitol

The ceiling and wall paintings of the Senate Appropriations Room (1857).
U.S. Capitol - executed the same year that construction the Church of Saint
Aloysius began.

The fresco design for the ceiling of the Senate Library (1857).

"Liberty, Peace, Plenty, War" (1859).
Senate Reception Room, marble figures, oil on plaster.

"Religion, William Brewster, Americus Vespucius, Executive (Authority),
Liberty, Christopher Columbus, Benjamin Franklin, Legislation."
All fresco with tempera borders of the President's Room.

Among many works abroad

The Frescos in the Church of the Madonna dell' Archetto (1850), Rome

The Decorative Chapel of the Torlonia Family (Villa Torlonia, Rome),
where he painted a frieze with the glory of Constantine and the family coat
of arms (1836).

Decorative Chapel of the Torlonia Family (Villa Torlonia, Rome)

The decoration of a gothic chapel in the park of the Villa di Porta Pia, Rome.

The restoration of the eleventh bay and end wall dedicated to Pope Gregory XVI in the third Loggia of the Vatican Palace (1840), Rome.

An honorary lithograph and portrait for the appointment of Pope Pius IX (1847).

The fifteen oil portrait studies of each pope as models on the frieze of St. Paul's Outside the Walls (1851 to 1872), Rome.

The painting of the Holy Trinity (1854), Cathedral in Mexico City.

Detail, "The Two Trinities"

It is in 1854 that Brumidi makes his decision to come back to Washington to begin his real artistic lifetime dream work in America. In this stage of his artistic journey, Brumidi completed other significant paintings in Catholic Jesuit American Churches:

'The Mystical Vision of St. Ignatius at La Sorta" (1856), Altar Painting, St. Ignatius Church, Baltimore, MD.

Murals in Immaculate Conception Church (1856), Boston, MA.

"Holy Trinity with Holy Family, in Egypt" a.k.a. "The Two Trinities" (1868). Gifted to Woodstock College, MD., now in St. Aloysuis Church, Wash. D.C.

Detail, "Two Trinities" Painting

"Madonna della Sedia" (copy of Raphael's oil) (1856), Oil, in the collection of Mr. and Mrs. Robert F. Young.

"God the Father and Dove of the Holy Spirit" (1863).

"Assumption of Blessed Virgin Mary" dome painting. Frescos, Cathedral Basilica of SS. Peter and Paul, New York.

"Crucifixion", altarpiece St. Stephen's Church New York City (1863).

"Crucifixion" by Brumidi

"Madonna and Child with St. Francis and St. Roche" leading away the European plague (1856),* Student Chapel, Gonzaga College H.S., Washington., D.C.

"Apparition of Our Lord to St. Margaret Mary," (1878). Painted originally for the Chapel of Visitation Convent, Wash., D.C.

* During Fr. Bernard Dooley's time as President of Gonzaga College High School, a gift of Brumidi's oil sketch for a larger work depicting the Assumption of Our Lady was presented to the school. It hangs now in Gonzaga's Student Chapel (same oil sketch that includes St, Francis and St. Roche).

Contributors

James Sanders, Photographer

This book is James Sander's first photographic portrayal of the structural elements of a church building. The entire body of his work vividly shows selected parts in the story of a building in the mid-1800's that came to be a portion of a guideline for other architects who were determining the architecture style and the growth of public buildings in the Federal City of Washington.

James has professionally done formal portrait work and photography of special events for several years. This particular effort to create photos that accentuate and portray the more poetical aspects of a structure has presented him with an artistic challenge.

Telling the story of Saint Aloysius Church in photography demanded a poetic sensibility of a visual artist like James. He says that this project was a working spiritual experience and awakening.

Nathan Leibowitz, Fine Artist/Illustrator

Nathan Leibowitz, a Philadelphia native, lives and works in the Metropolitan Washington Area.

Currently, he is an Associate Artist at the Torpedo Art Factory in Alexandria, Virginia. His finely executed architectural drawings are the results of extensive guidance by his father, Lanny Louis Leibotwitz, a noted architect in Philadelphia. Nathan employs a high degree of technique to create beautiful, stylized and intricate renderings with the use of fine penman-

Nathan Leibowitz, Graphics Illustrator and James Sanders, Photographer

ship, stippling and hatching approaches. In addition to private showings, Nathan has successfully participated in more formal exhibits at the American Horticultural Society's "River Farm" location near Mount Vernon, Virginia. Nathan also claims his work on the Saint Aloysius Church book project was a motivating spiritual experience.

Ryan P. Connell

This book was made more possible by the technical assistance of Ryan P. Connell who guided me meticulously in the structuring and production of the manuscript for submission to New Academia Publishing. Ryan is also greatly responsible for shaping and refining the visuals to fit the text as well as providing some photos of his own.

Robert Francis Murray, Author

Bob is a '53 graduate of Gonzaga College High School and of Georgetown University, BLS '76, MALS, 1991. He is an active member in the Former Jesuits, Novitiate of St. Isaac Jogues (now The Jesuit Center), 1954 to 1958.; associated with the Georgetown Office of Scholarly Publications in connection with the writing of Swampoodle Lily; author of Gonzaga Memories, 1917-1990. Founder and Director of the von Brahler Ltd./Gallery ,1983 to 2011, its main concern being the work and concerns of living, Russian-born artists; Founder of The Association of Alexandria Art Galleries, the AAAG, (1985 to-1995); contributing art reporter and writer to the Zebra, regional monthly newspaper, Alexandria and Arlington 66,000 circulation.
Presently, Bob continues to exhibit his own "Waterexpressions" in local art venues and online. Born in Danville, PA, 1935, he resides with wife of 50+ years, Rosemary Griffin Murray, in the Mount Vernon Area, Alexandria, Virginia.

Awarded a Doctorate of Humane Letters (LHD) by Gonzaga College in 1995 for contribution to Alumni programs in the creation of seven art memorials in the Gonzaga campus complex and for dedication to his role to the Planning and Work on the St. Aloysius Church Renovation, '91 to '94.

"Rising," by James Sanders

Acknowledgements

This book is dedicated in gratitude to the untiring efforts of the members of the Saint Aloysius Church Renovation Planning and Working Committees, 1991-1994, namely, Fr. Dooley, Fr. Lingan, Fr. Novotny, John Delaney, Frank Duane, Stu Long, Terry Matan and Bob Thuman and to all future members of Committees for the Continuing Care, Preservation and Use of the Church Building.

Special deep thanks to the current President of Gonzaga, Fr. Stephen Planning, S.J. and Team for the recent major improvements to the exterior and for overseeing the repair of the church roof severely damaged by a violent storm.

I could not have completed this book project without the years of prompting and encouragement by Anne Ridder, former Assistant Dean, Georgetown Liberal Studies Program and the mentorship by Carole Sargent, Founding Director of the Office of Scholarly Publications, Georgetown University, Washington, D.C. and her devoted team of Faculty Book Groups.

A lifetime of gratitude to Rosemary, my wife, for her untiring transcription of materials, close scrutiny to detail and care for all that is worthwhile.

There would be no book now in hand without the acceptance, wisdom, patience and tutelage of Anna Lawton, New Academia Publishing.

Bibliography

Ambassy, Emilio. *Architecture of Luis Barragan, Chapel for Capuchines, Tiapen, New Mexico.* New York: Museum of Modern Art, 1976, 1984.

Ashihara, Yoshinova. *Exterior Design in Architecture.* New York: Van Nostrand Reinhold Co., 1970.

Barron, Robert. *Heaven in Stone and Glass.* Wernersville, PA: The Jesuit Center Library, 2002.

Branner, Robert. *Great Ages of World Architecture:Gothic Architecture.* New York: George Braziller, 1961/1982.

Bulletin, St. Aloysius Church, Vol. 1, 1904; Vol. 5, 1909. Washington, DC: Gonzaga Archives.

Burden, Ernest, *Architectural Delineation.* New York: McGraw-Hill Book Co., 1991.

Campbell, James W.P. *Building St. Paul's.* London: Thames & Hudson Publishers, 2008.

Carrington, James. *Visual Art, Critical Introduction.* New York: Harcourt Brace Jovanovich, 1982.

Ciaga, Graziella Leyla. *Cathedrals of the World.* Verielle, Italy: Whitestar Publishers, 2006.

Conrad, Peter. *Modern Times, Modern Places.* New York: Alfred A. Knopp, Inc., 1968.

Day, Christopher. *Places of the Soul, Architecture and Environmental Design as a Healing Art.* London: The Aquarian Press, 1990.

Delbanca, Nicholas. *Lastingnesss.* New York: Grand Central Publishing, 2001.

Drekmann, Godfrey, O.S.B. *Church Architecture, The Shape of Reform, The Reformed Liturgy.* Washington, D.C.: The Liturgical Conference, 1965.

DuFief, M. M. *Dissertation: A History of Saint Aloysius Parish 1859-1909.* Washington, DC: Georgetown University, 1960.

Edwards, Betty. *Drawing on the Artist Within.* New York: Touchstone, 1986

Feldman, Edmund Burke. "Architecture of Internal Space," *Varieties of Visual Experience,* Chapter 12. Englewood Cliffs, N.J.: Prentice Hall, Inc., 1972.

Follett, Ken. *Pillars of the Almighty.* Photos by F. Step Fitzgerald. New York: William Morrow & Co., Inc., 1994.

Gonzaga College – 1821-1921. Centennial Volume. Washingon, DC: Gonzaga College, 1921.

Haneman, John Theodore. *Historic Architectural Plans, Details and Elements*. New York: Dover Publications, Inc., 1984.

Hoffman, Malvina. *Sculpture, Inside and Out.* Chapters IV, V. New York: Bonanza Books, 1939.

Jacobs, David, *Architecture.* New York: Newsweek, 1974.

Jung, Carl G., M.L. Frony, Joseph L. Henderson, Jolande Jacobi and Amelia Jaffe, eds. *Man and His Symbols.* Garden City, N.Y.: Windfall Book, Double Day and Co., Inc., 1964.

Kornetchuk, Elena. *The Quest for Self Expression: Painting in Moscow and Leningrad 1965-1990*, Exhibition Catalog. Columbus, Ohio: Columbus Museum of Art, 1991.

Lucas, Thomas M., S.J. *Landmarking, City, Church & Jesuit Urban Strategy.* Chicago: Loyola Press, 1998.

_____, ed. *Spirit, Style, Story*. Essays honoring John W. Padberg, S.J. Chicago: Loyola Press, 1990.

Lynch, Kevin. *Site Planning.* Cambridge, MA: M.I.T. Press, 1914.

Metcalf, Paul. *Waters of the Potomack*, Charlottesville, VA: University of Virginia, 1982.

Miele, Chris, ed. "Wm. Morrison Architecture," *The Story of the Unknown Church, Architecture and History.* Sheffield, England: Sheffield Academic Press, 1996.

Mueller, G. Martin. Jr. "AIA Guide," *The Architecture of Washington.* Baltimore, MD: Johns Hopkins University Press, 2006.

New Catholic Encyclopedia. Prepared by an Editorial Staff at the Catholic University of America. New York: McGraw-Hill Book Company, 1967.

Placzek, Adolf K. *The Four Books of Architecture.* New introduction by Andrew Palladio. New York: Columbia University Dover Publications, Inc., 1965.

Rose, Michael. *Ugly as Sin.* Bedford, NH: Sophia Institute Press, 2001.

St. Aloysius Church, The Jubilee Program, 1858-1934. Washington, D.C.: W.F. Roberts Co, 1934.

Stemp, Richard. *The Secret Language of Churches and Cathedrals; Decoding the Sacred Symbolism of Christianity's Holy Buildings.* London : Duncan Baird Publications, 2001.

The Catholic Historical Review, October 1990, Vol. I, XX, No. 4. CITY: Washington, DC: The Catholic University Press of America.

Weller, Charles E. *Neglected Neighbors: Stories of Life in the Alleys, Tenements and Shanties of the Nation's Capital, 1909/1923*, London: Forgotten Books, 2017.

Wolanin, Barbara A. *Constantino Brumidi, Artist of the Capitol.* Washington, D.C.: U.S. Government Printing Office, 1998.

Young, Bonnie. *A Walk Through the Cloisters*, photos by Malcom Veron. New York: The Metropolitan Museum of Art, 1979.

CPSIA information can be obtained
at www.ICGtesting.com
Printed in the USA
BVHW022043110919
558006BV00004B/2/P

* 9 7 8 0 9 9 9 5 5 7 2 8 0 *